YOUR MAKER'S
MISSION

Ben Melancon

YOUR MAKER'S
MISSION

Partnering with God's
heart for the Nations

Ben
Melancon

Published by: ADVANTAGE BOOKS™
                  Longwood, FL
                  www.advbookstore.com

Library of Congress Catalog Number: 2021942491

Names:	Melancon, Ben
Title:	Your Maker's Mission / Ben Melancon
Description	Longwood: Advantage Books, 2021
Identifiers:	ISBN (print): 9781597556187, (mobi, epub): 9781597556279
Catgory:	RELIGION: Christian Ministry – Missions
	RELIGION: Christian Ministry – Evangelism
Subjects:	Missions; Christian Missions Books; Christian Mission; Worldwide Evangelism; World Evangelism; Funding World Evangelism; World Evangelism Mission

First Printing: August 2021
21 22 23 24 25 26   10 9 8 7 6 5 4 3 2 1

Table of Contents

Ben Melancon

Part 1
God's Story

Ben Melancon

Chapter 1

No One Came to Tell Us

"No one came to tell us." This sentence from a young Kenyan man, spoken years ago, continues to echo in my mind. Christian missionaries came to his home village in northern Kenya to share the gospel by way of the Jesus film. With joy radiating from his eyes, his smile, and the tone in his voice, he shared that he heard and received the good news of salvation in Jesus. Summing up the story, he told me he would have received Jesus as his Savior earlier if someone had come and told him.

Another anecdote also stays with me: "One of my good friends spent time recently among unreached and unengaged peoples in Southeast Asia. As he talked with villagers in one remote area, he tried to uncover their core beliefs. He asked them, 'How were we created?' They responded, 'We don't know.' He asked, 'Who sends the rain for the crops?' They responded, 'We don't know that either.' Then he asked, 'What happens when we die?' They looked back at him and said, 'No one has come to tell us about that yet.' Soon thereafter, he found himself in another remote village with people who had never heard the gospel. They were warm and hospitable, and they invited him to share a drink with them. One man went into his small shop and reappeared moments later with a classic red Coke can. Immediately, it hit home with my friend. A soft-drink company in Atlanta has done a better job getting brown sugar water to these people than the church of Jesus Christ has done in getting the gospel to them."[1] No one has come to share the eternally refreshing gospel of the kingdom, yet an Atlanta Company selling sugar water has been successful in giving them temporary refreshment.

These stories stay with me because there are multitudes of men and women from thousands of villages and cities who have yet to hear the good news of

---

[1] David Platt, *Radical: Taking Back Your Faith from the American Dream*, (The Crown Publishing Group, Kindle Edition), 158-159.

Jesus Christ and there is no one among them to tell them. There is no one present to tell them and no Bible for them to read. Imagine mountains and valleys, large expanses of land speckled with villages and cities, where eternal souls remain weary and burdened, without hope, devoid of fellowship with their Maker. Imagine you are one of them. Sit back for a moment or take a walk in the near future, putting yourself in their shoes in light of the salvation you have because of the rich mercy of God. You possess the greatest gift that can ever be given to a person. And you are given the privilege to share this free gift with others, as it was shared with you.

Ponder this: Why have you received salvation in Jesus, yet still live on earth in a body that is fading away? What is the purpose of your ongoing existence in a world that is at war with its Maker? Having received Jesus, you now possess eternal life in God and if you die right now, you are victorious. If you pass from your physical body in this moment, you are with the Lord in your spirit. When Jesus returns, you will be reunited with your body and be immortal. It is better by far to be with the Lord than to continue on in this life, as Paul writes: "For to me, to live is Christ, and to die is gain. But if I live on in the flesh, this will mean fruit from my labor; yet what I shall choose I cannot tell. For I am hard-pressed between the two, having a desire to depart and be with Christ, which is far better" (Philippians 1:21-23). It is far better to depart from this present body and evil age to be with Christ, so what is the purpose of your remaining? Your purpose is fellowship with God and inviting others into the same fellowship wherever you journey with Jesus.

With the above thoughts in mind, I invite you to give yourself fully to the most important and significant mission in our day. This mission marches forward with two thousand years of rich history, beckoning for Christ-filled laborers until it is complete. The most heroic men and women of every generation since its inception fill its ranks. It has and will continue to be the preeminent justice movement in all of the earth from heaven's perspective. The activities of this movement and all those involved will be remembered forever. The effects of this movement will bring about lasting peace in every place on earth. All are invited into the mission with none being disqualified if they simply say yes to its Leader and join Him in their part.

The One who is leading this mission has all necessary credentials to bring it to full completion. He owns all things, all was made through Him, is sustained by Him, and all things will be restored because of Him (Colossians 1:15-20). There is no other of His caliper. As one song articulates:

You have no rival, You have no equal
Now and forever, God, You reign
Yours is the Kingdom, Yours is the glory
Yours is the Name, above all names
What a powerful Name it is
What a powerful Name it is
The Name of Jesus Christ my King[2]

He is fully divine in nature while also fully man. He is completely God and human. The Bible calls this the mystery of godliness (1 Timothy 3:16). To lead the world back to enduring righteousness, justice, and peace that was lost near its start requires a sacrifice and only God can be that sacrifice by becoming a person (1 John 1:1-3; 2:1-2; Romans 5:12-15). He gave His life for the mission's success. The mission marches triumphantly forward through His church because He lives forever by His resurrection from the dead (Hebrews 5:8; 7:24-25). His name is Jesus Christ, He has been given all authority in heaven and on earth, and He is unstoppable.

The Old Testament speaks of Him often and with the highest regard. Consider Isaiah 52:13-15:

[13]*Behold, My Servant [Jesus] shall deal prudently; He shall be exalted and extolled and be very high.* [14]*Just as many were astonished at you, So His visage was marred more than any man, And His form more than the sons of men;* [15]*So shall He sprinkle many nations. Kings shall shut their mouths at Him; For what had not been told them they shall see, And what they had not heard they shall consider.*

Carried by the Holy Spirit, prophets spoke of Jesus as One who stands alone in beauty and wonder. He is high and holy with the names Wonderful, Counselor, Mighty God, Everlasting Father, and Prince of Peace while also being gentle and lowly, depicted as a lamb sacrificed for the sins of the world. He is declared to be a ruler coming out of the small town of Bethlehem, Israel,

---

[2] "What a Beautiful Name." Ben Fielding and Brooke Ligertwood, 2015.

who is from everlasting while simultaneously being crushed for the world's iniquities. He is the child prophesied to arise from humanity, bringing blessing to all nations.

The child is God's only begotten Son who asks for all the nations as His inheritance and the ends of the earth as His possession (Psalm 2:8). A global resistance arises against this request, continuing to this day (Psalm 2:1-3). Undaunted, He asks the Father confidently and people from every tribe are receiving His desire for them and becoming His inheritance. His dream is to have all nations as His inheritance. He began a mission that will touch every tribe on earth. The mission is to go to every people group, preach the gospel of the kingdom, and make disciples (Matthew 28:18-20). The movement continues through His ambassadors who have received Him. They go with Him, compelled by His love. His dream will be fulfilled.

Some from all nations will receive the message of the gospel, fulfilling the dream. Jesus declared: "This gospel of the kingdom will be preached in all the world as a witness to all the nations, and then the end will come" (Matthew 24:14). John the apostle saw this ahead of time: "After these things I looked, and behold, a great multitude which no one could number, of all nations, tribes, peoples, and tongues, standing before the throne and before the Lamb [Jesus], clothed with white robes, with palm branches in their hands, and crying out with a loud voice, saying, 'Salvation belongs to our God who sits on the throne, and to the Lamb!'" (Revelation 7:9-10). The gospel will be preached to all nations, and some from all nations, tribes, peoples, and tongues will declare that salvation belongs to God who sits on the throne and to the Lamb.

What does Jesus mean by "all the nations"? As a part of the body of Christ, we should grapple with this since we are given a mission and that mission is fulfilled through our partnership with Jesus. He spoke of the gospel being preached to all nations and making disciples of all nations (Matthew 24:14; 28:19). In these passages, the original Greek word for nations is *ethnos*. The word *ethnic* is used in English. It means any non-Jew and it can also mean individuals who share a common identity, such as a language. There can be many such groups within one country's present political boundaries. For example, Nigeria is one nation, yet it contains within its borders hundreds of distinct people groups (nations/*ethnos*) with different languages.

People who study missions labor to bring clarity to what the phrase "all the nations" means. For *ethnos*, some use the term *people group,* which is used throughout this book. By people group, I mean: "a significantly large grouping of individuals who perceive themselves to have a common affinity for one another because of their shared language, religion, ethnicity, residence, occupation, class or caste, situation, etc., or combinations of these."[3] There are thousands of people groups in the earth based on this definition. There are different numbers of people groups dependent on various factors used in determining them, like language and caste. Joshua Project, a Christian organization whose aim is to bring definition to the unfinished task, explains their research on this. For the sake of simplicity, their count is used in this book. Their estimate of ethnic people groups globally is around 17,000. This list uses language, in addition to religion, caste, and culture. They use this count "for evangelistic purposes" of declaring the gospel to "all the nations." This comes from the Lausanne Committee Chicago meeting from 1982: "For evangelization purposes, a people group is the largest group within which the Gospel can spread as a church planting movement without encountering barriers of understanding or acceptance."[4]

The 17,000 ethnic people groups divide into reached and unreached people groups. Approximately 7,000 are considered unreached, roughly 40% of the total of all people groups. An unreached people group is "a people group in which there is no indigenous community of believing Christians able to evangelize this people group."[5] Consulting together in the 1990s, mission strategists settled on the criteria for an unreached people group as less than 2% Christ followers. The idea here is that a minimum of 2% of a culture having a vision for change is needed to lead to changing the whole culture. This does not prove true in every situation but is simply a marker to help give definition to the unfinished task of declaring the gospel to all people groups.

---

[3] "Has Everyone Heard?"
https://joshuaproject.net/resources/articles/has_everyone_heard.
[4] "How Many People Groups Are There?"
https://joshuaproject.net/resources/articles/ how_many_people_groups_are_there.
[5] Ibid.

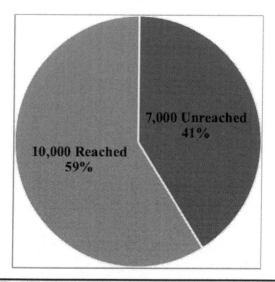

Ethnos (nations): Individuals who share a common identity, such as a language; can be hundreds of these distinct groups within one country's borders.
People group: Can be interchangeable with ethnos; significantly large grouping of individuals who perceive themselves to have a common affinity for one another because of shared language, religion, ethnicity, residence, occupation, class or caste, situation, etc., or combinations of these.
Unreached people group: People group in which there is no indigenous community of Christ followers able to evangelize the group; less than 2% of the group is evangelical.

Following are two examples of unreached people groups: The Dhobi people in India have a population of around twelve million. They are among India's Dalit community, formerly known as the "untouchables." They are low in the caste system and wash clothes for higher castes. They bow to a washing stone as their forefathers did. The majority worship Hindu gods.[6] The Chut-Ruc people in Laos have a population of around 200. They live high in the mountains of central Laos on the Vietnamese border. Joshua Project states, "If someone is bitten by a tiger, bear, or snake, the Ruc believe them to be cursed. They are not allowed to return to their village for two or three months. The person must live deep within the forest for this time and cannot be visited by friends or relatives. Ancestor worship is not practiced in each Ruc home but is only observed in the home of the village chief. The Ruc also believe in a hierarchy of spirits of which the earth, humans, animals, and the

---

[6] "Dhobi (Hindu traditions) in India,"
https://joshuaproject.net/people_groups/16709/IN.

forest are considered the most powerful. There is no record of Christians ever having focused on the Ruc in Laos with the Gospel. They are completely unreached."[7]

The vast majority of unreached people groups live in the 10/40 window. The 10/40 window is a large area of land that covers parts of North Africa, the Middle East, and Asia (see the rectangle in the image below). The name comes from latitude lines that define the area, approximately between 10 degrees north and 40 degrees north. This window holds two-thirds of our global population. Out of the 17,000 people groups on earth, 7,000 are considered unreached. Of the 7,000 unreached people groups, around 6,000 live in the 10/40 window. The top 50 least evangelized megacities (with populations over one million) are found there. The majority of the world's poor live in the 10/40 window.[8] In summary, of the 40% of the world's population that is comprised of unreached peoples, around 85% of those unreached peoples live in the 10/40 window. So this area of the world must be a main focus of the church if we are to finish Jesus' mission with Him.

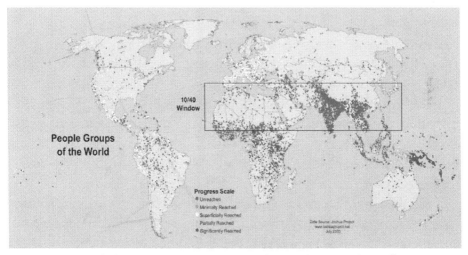

"Great Commission Maps," https://joshuaproject.net/resources/maps.[9]

---

[7] " Chut-Ruc in Laos," http://joshuaproject.net/people_groups/14586/LA.
[8] "What is the 10/40 Window?"
https://joshuaproject.net/resources/articles/10_40_window.
[9] "Great Commission Maps," https://joshuaproject.net/resources/maps.

Around 2,000 years ago, Jesus conferred His mission on His church to complete with Him. He is not discouraged by the above figures. People from every people group will hear the good news of the kingdom and receive His love for them. The gospel of the kingdom spread to around 60% of the earth's people groups over two millennia. The remaining 40% will hear it prior to Jesus' return (Matthew 24:14; Acts 28:28). 60% of the earth heard the gospel over 2,000 years. 40% could hear it in the span of a generation or two when considering several factors. The signs Jesus spoke of in Matthew 24 are happening increasingly on a global scale, and global wickedness is increasing. In this context, Jesus says the gospel of the kingdom will be preached in all nations (Matthew 24:14). Various Christian organizations speak of the gospel reaching every people group in the next decade or two. This means we will see the Spirit poured out, along with an increase in workers going to these remaining peoples as the world has not yet seen. We are privileged to live in a time when the mission will be completed.

What has been spoken of by God from near the beginning of creation is nearing its time of fulfillment. The ongoing message from the courts of heaven is that all nations will turn to the Lord. This is now made possible by Jesus' sacrifice, His resurrection from the dead, and the outpouring of the Holy Spirit (Acts 2:17-21). Though missionary endeavors into the 10/40 window have been low when compared to endeavors among already reached peoples, and though the movement of finances has been startlingly minuscule toward reaching the unreached, this is changing and will continue to change. Workers are going and will saturate the 10/40 window, and finances will back them to do the work of declaring the gospel of the kingdom to every remaining unreached people.

Jesus' desire for all nations has not changed. Thus, His final instructions have not changed—unto having all nations as His inheritance. So we are still going with Him into all the world, preaching the gospel and making disciples (Mark 16:15-16; Matthew 28:18-20). The call goes out from heaven, "Whom shall I send, and who will go for Us?" (Isaiah 6:8), while tribes on earth call out, "Come over and help us" (Acts 16:9). Heaven looks for ambassadors to send. Tribes wait for those ambassadors to come. If we do not focus on this primary mission, we miss out on a significant part of His heart. We do not all go, but we are all to seek first His kingdom and His righteousness (Matthew

6:33). And His desire is for His kingdom to be declared to all people groups. Our focus on the mission does not always equate to going to unreached peoples, but it certainly means making abiding in Jesus our priority, affecting how we spend time, money, and resources, playing our part with Him in the mission He is leading.

This book is written to biblically tell God's eternal love story, the mission He gives us, and ways we can be involved in His mission. He has told us His story, which is presently unfolding, in His word. In the Old Testament, He gives promises that show us where His story is going and His heart motivation that moves His story forward. In the New Testament, He shows us the fulfillment of His promises in Jesus Christ and the template He gives us for accomplishing His mission with Him. Those who place their trust in Jesus are part of the fulfillment of the eternal Maker's promises and are invited to partner with Him for their completion. Knowing the love of Christ compels us to be on His mission with Him, seeking first His kingdom and His righteousness.

Father in heaven, reveal Your story to me. Let me see Your mission clearly and direct me to my part in Your story.

Throughout the remainder of Part 1, we will look at God's eternal love story as described in His Word.

Ben Melancon

Chapter 2

The Beginning

We each a have a story that is deeper than we comprehend. The story of a person's life is not primarily about events that come and go, nor is it about outward appearance. It is a combination of many things, including relationships, culture(s) a person lives within, family background, and education, shaping each journey. Each person's story, though unique, is formed through and entwined with the stories of others. From all these things and more there have occurred wounds and healings, victories and defeats, with emotions and desires fulfilled and unfulfilled. We are more than outward appearance and deeper than we understand—for we came from an eternal source.

Without a story, unfolding along a journey, there are no markers to show us where we came from or where we are going. Jeff Goins spoke about the power of story in this way:

> Story is where we came from. Story is where we're going. Story is what connects us and binds us to each other. It is in the story of humanity, amongst love and fear and failure, that we make meaning of our lives.
>
> Story is what defines us and sets us apart. It's what allows us to connect with each other, to truly know and *be* known.
>
> Story is powerful.
>
> Story is grossly misunderstood.
>
> A good story has conflict, but ultimately resolves. A story is messy and full of confusion, but there is meaning and completeness to it. A story is about people and places, not ideas and concepts.

Stories are concrete, absolute, and certain. Yet, they are *mysterious*. Stories have natural momentum to them, fueling our passion to find out more from the teller.

Stories are laden with bait and intrigue, with suspense and tension. Stories are *provocative*.[11]

As each person has a story, so does God, our Creator. His story is unique. It is without rival. His story is preeminent because He is without equal. All our stories, entwined with each other are within the bounds of His grand story. He shares His story with us in His word, the Bible. It contains a wonderful beginning, a conflict, and beautiful resolution that never ends. Provoking, it identifies and stirs up within the human heart the deepest desire behind our existence—fellowship with our Maker. In this chapter, we will look at who God is as the author of the story, how creation came out of God's nature, and humanity's role in God's creation.

The author behind creation, God, is eternal light, life, and love. He created from His wholehearted love. This love manifested with light that brought forth life. There was no darkness, death, or hatred in the mix when God made the heavens, the earth, the sea, and all things and beings in them. As humans living in a world where these things are the norm, we have no grid for what life would be like without them, save what God's word recounts and promises to restore. What has been normal for us is moth and rust destroying, things fading away, and plants, animals, and people dying. The earth will be restored to its original state by the same word of light, life, and love that spoke it into existence.

God is light and there is no darkness in Him at all (1 John 1:5). The first manifestation of the creation of the heavens and earth was light (Genesis 1:3). God divided the light from the darkness (Genesis 1:4). This "light" came prior to the sun, moon, and stars (Genesis 1:14). This original light and darkness is not the light and darkness that we physically see. Looking at the story of God, the light is a person with a nature who has no darkness in Him. This "spiritual light" and nature of God motivated, produced, and filled creation. Creation,

---

[11] Jeff Goins, "Goins, Writer," *Why I Believe in the Power of Story*, http://goinswriter.com/power-of-story.

including people, were separated from this light when Adam and Eve chose to lead themselves apart from God. God reveals this light of Himself through Jesus, His only begotten Son, to bring us back into His light—into fellowship with Him (John 1:4; 8:12; 2 Corinthians 4:4, 6). All creation came forth from this light and is being restored to it. When Jesus returns, those who received His light will shine like the sun in the kingdom of their Father (John 8:12; Matthew 13:43).

God is eternal life: life without beginning and without end. His life is more than physical life—it is eternal existence with eternal pleasure (Psalm 16:11). This life of God filled creation. The absence of the life of God entered creation when Adam and Eve, God's image-bearers, chose to attempt life apart from Him. Life continued, but in a lesser state than the Maker intended. God's invitation back to eternal life is through Jesus Christ (John 17:3). He is the eternal life in flesh, who made all things, upholds all things by the word of His power, and is appointed to reign over all forever (Hebrews 1:2-3; 1 John 1:1-2). His life is light for humanity (John 1:4). Apart from His life, people cannot see properly, in a spiritual sense. Those who receive the life of Jesus before He returns receive His eternal life now, internally. When He returns, they will receive immortal bodies and reign with Him forever in a new (restored) heavens and earth (1 Corinthians 15:50-57; Revelation 5:9-10).

God spoke "Let there be light" and breathed His life into man out of His love. He is love (1 John 4:8, 16). His story flows out of the heart of His eternal love and delight. As the heavens and earth and everything in them continued in a diminished light and life apart from humanity's fellowship with God, so people could no longer live in love toward God or others apart from God. This is evidenced immediately after Adam and Eve's rejection of God when Adam blamed Eve for his sin. A little further along, murder entered with Cain and Abel. This progressed until the hearts of people were continually on evil, leading up to the flood in Noah's time. Like light and life, God makes His love known by Jesus Christ laying down His life for us (1 John 3:16). (We will look at why this is important in the next chapters when the conflict is examined.) God has eternally loved Himself among Himself as the Father, Son, and Holy Spirit. Before creation existed as we know it, God was the same in His nature.

Creation is the display of God loving as Himself those He made. Jesus identified the two greatest commandments given from God as loving Him with our whole heart, mind, soul, and strength, and loving our neighbor as ourselves (Matthew 22:37-40). He made people out of His love, to love them. There was never a moment when God started loving His creation—He has eternally loved His creation. This is the motivation for people to love God with their everything, for this is how He loves us—with His all.

With humanity willfully stepping away from their Maker, they left behind His light, life, and love, and lived in agreement with lies. The effects of this have been ongoing darkness, death, and hatred. Jesus was sent to destroy the works of darkness and to give Himself to humanity for whosoever will receive, among all the tribes of the earth. He invites us back into the fellowship of light, life, and love, out of which He originally created. He beckons us out of the kingdom of darkness—a kingdom that outwardly may look appealing and valuable but is not eternally satisfying (1 John 2:15-16). The present world and its values are fading away, but those who do the will of God will abide forever in a new heavens and earth—the home of righteousness (1 John 2:17; 2 Peter 3:10-13).

People were made in God's image, for intimacy and dominion. Fellowship involves both of these. We were made to have a close, familial relationship with our Maker and to rule with Him in His nature, to abide in His love. God's goal for humanity is for us to humbly abide in His love and fill the earth with the knowledge of His love, leading to perpetual prospering in all of creation. Creation started in intimacy, with a blessing to multiply and have dominion. We look forward to when creation will be restored to this original model in light and love, free from darkness and death.

God created people to be like Him and to experience His pleasure. In the first chapter of Genesis, we find the account of God's decision and action to create people: "Then God said, 'Let Us make man in Our image, according to Our likeness; let them have dominion over the fish of the sea, over the birds of the air, and over the cattle, over all the earth and over every creeping thing that creeps on the earth.' So God created man in His own image; in the image of God He created him; male and female He created them" (Genesis 1:26-27). People are created as male and female in the image of God, to represent His essence—being holy as He is holy.

We were made in the image of the One who is full of joy with eternal pleasures. He crafted us as His very image, in delight and with rejoicing. True satisfaction is found only in relationship with our Maker. Knowing this leads to dominion that produces life rather than death.

Made in His image and to experience His pleasure, humans receive a blessing of multiplication and dominion from God. "Then God blessed them [Adam and Eve], and God said to them, 'Be fruitful and multiply; fill the earth and subdue it; have dominion over the fish of the sea, over the birds of the air, and over every living thing that moves on the earth'" (Genesis 1:28). They were given the privilege of governing creation with God. Through multiplication and dominion, the earth was to be filled with the knowledge of the glory of God as the water covers the sea. But a tragedy occurred with devastating effects.

We were created to fellowship with God. After a wonderful beginning to this fellowship, the offer to depart from fellowship came.

Ben Melancon

Chapter 3

Humanity's Rebellion

An oracle within my heart concerning the transgression of the wicked: There is no fear of God before his eyes. ²For he flatters himself in his own eyes When he finds out his iniquity and when he hates. ³The words of his mouth are wickedness and deceit; He has ceased to be wise and to do good. ⁴He devises wickedness on his bed; He sets himself in a way that is not good; He does not abhor evil.

⁵Your mercy, O LORD, is in the heavens; Your faithfulness reaches to the clouds. ⁶Your righteousness is like the great mountains; Your judgments are a great deep; O LORD, You preserve man and beast.

⁷How precious is Your lovingkindness, O God! Therefore the children of men put their trust under the shadow of Your wings. ⁸They are abundantly satisfied with the fullness of Your house, And You give them drink from the river of Your pleasures. ⁹For with You is the fountain of life; In Your light we see light.

¹⁰Oh, continue Your lovingkindness to those who know You, And Your righteousness to the upright in heart. ¹¹Let not the foot of pride come against me, And let not the hand of the wicked drive me away. ¹²There the workers of iniquity have fallen; They have been cast down and are not able to rise. (Psalm 36)

This Psalm expresses two truths resulting from human departure from fellowship with the Creator. First, they sought to lead themselves without God. This aim brought about the degrading of others rather than living together in love and unity. Then, amidst their rebellion, God pursued them with His mercy, faithfulness, righteousness, and justice. Though humanity is guilty, the Lord reaches toward them in their hiding and growing wickedness.

The beginning was fellowship in perfection, then the cunning enemy offered a different way of existence. He invites Eve to agree with lies rather than staying in the truth. In a conflict of loyalties, a choice is made that brings about devastating effects for all of creation. In this chapter we will observe the new character in the plot: the enemy, as well as humanity's agreement with this enemy's deception, and the ensuing consequences.

While all was beauty and delight between God and people in Eden, the enemy lurked, waiting for an opportune time to seduce God's image-bearers. Creation is completed with God, as the protagonist, delighting in humanity and humanity resting in His delight as they tend the Garden of Eden. Adam and Eve possess the life of God, He gives them dominion over His creation, and He comes and fellowships with them (Genesis 2:7; 3:8). The antagonist, Satan, approaches Eve. The Lord God told Adam previously, "Of every tree of the garden you may freely eat; but of the tree of the knowledge of good and evil you shall not eat, for in the day that you eat of it you shall surely die" (Genesis 2:16b-17). In direct opposition against God, Satan seeks to take the dominion given to Adam and Eve by seducing them to go against what God said. Ultimately, his aim is to subvert God Himself.

Satan was not originally a murderer and father of lies. God created Satan without evil. He was an anointed cherub in God's court, beautiful and filled with wisdom (Ezekiel 28:12-15). Cherubs are winged creatures, in close proximity to God's throne. In the Tabernacle of Moses, which is a copy of the heavenly tabernacle, two cherubs were in the Holy of Holies, on top of the Ark of the Covenant, overshadowing the mercy seat. Like the two cherubs, Satan was in the presence of the mercy of God. As an anointed cherub, Satan was perfect in his ways when God created him. Then unrighteousness was found in him.

Satan's unrighteousness produced his rage against God and His image-bearers. Satan began to look at himself, admiring his beauty, power, and wisdom. Idolizing God's gifts to him, he began to think of himself apart from God. Choosing to worship himself brought desire to be worshipped, even by His Maker. This meant he needed to overtake his Maker's throne. His initial path to this was to gain dominion over the earth by getting God's image-bearers, to whom the Maker had given dominion over the earth, to take the same path of unrighteousness. He is the one identified as the serpent in Genesis 3 (2 Corinthians 11:3, 14; Revelation 20:2). With wickedness brewing in his heart, Eve became his initial target.

Satan deceived Eve by way of lies, slander, and accusation. There are various names used for Satan throughout the Scriptures, a few of them being the serpent, the dragon, the evil one, a prowling lion, and the devil (Matthew 6:13; John 8:44; 1 Peter 5:8; Revelation 20:2). These names hold in them ideas of lying, slandering, accusing, killing, and destroying. Genesis 3:1-5 gives the dialogue between the serpent and Eve:

Now the serpent was more cunning than any beast of the field which the LORD God had made. And he said to the woman, "Has God indeed said, 'You shall not eat of every tree of the garden?'" ²And the woman said to the serpent, "We may eat the fruit of the trees of the garden; ³but of the fruit of the tree which is in the midst of the garden, God has said, 'You shall not eat it, nor shall you touch it, lest you die.'" ⁴Then the serpent said to the woman, "You will not surely die. ⁵For God knows that in the day you eat of it your eyes will be opened, and you will be like God, knowing good and evil.

Satan lied to Eve by contradicting what God said: namely, that she and Adam would not die if they ate of the tree. He slandered God's goodness by falsely promising that, if Adam and Eve partook of the tree, they would get something wonderful that they were missing. Satan accused the Lord God of withholding good from His image-bearers. The serpent did all of this, though he did not create humans, does not care to fellowship with them in love, and provides nothing for them, while God in His love spoke the truth to them and blessed them with life, light, and dominion.

Now that new ideas were before them, Adam and Eve chose. "So when the woman saw that the tree was good for food, that it was pleasant to the eyes, and a tree desirable to make one wise, she took of its fruit and ate. She also gave to her husband with her, and he ate" (Genesis 3:6). Adam agreed with the lies, directly or indirectly, as he ate with Eve. Eve interpreted Satan's words as an appeal to taste and touch beauty, in order to be wise. Adam and Eve believed this and took the fruit, not remaining in the truth that they were made in the image of the One who is the perfection of wisdom and beauty. Their choice revealed their loyalty and determined their destiny.

Adam and Eve got to choose for or against fellowship with their Maker. Why would God make them in such a way, knowing there are eternal implications? He did not have to make them—He desired to. He voluntarily made them in His image, as eternal beings. As the Eternal One, He made them by choice out of His whole heart, with hearts to choose independence by self-rule or dependence by humble fellowship. The implications are eternal because God is eternal and we are made in His likeness. The Maker's purpose for forming people in His image is not to have rule followers, but voluntary lovers who delight to abide in His eternal benevolence and pleasure.

Concerning choice and its implications, the earth's first inhabitants chose to be wise in their own eyes, departing from fellowship with their Maker (Genesis 3:6). They made their decision willingly, rebelling against their Maker. Reasoning that the tree had the ability to make them wise apart from God, they ate. Solomon seems to look back to this event when he wrote, "Do not be wise in your own eyes; Fear the LORD and depart from evil" (Proverbs 3:7), and, "When pride comes, then comes shame; But with the humble is wisdom" (Proverbs 11:2). They exchanged the life of God in and with them for the way of independence. Choosing their own wisdom, they departed from true goodness, and all that remained was life apart from God: evil and humanity's attempt to be good in their own strength and by their own definition. Another way to say life apart from God is "dead in trespasses and sins" (Ephesians 2:1).

Immediately, effects of Adam and Eve's choice became evident. Before being deceived, they were naked and unashamed. After, they realized something went tragically wrong. Their eyes opened to consequences of their choice, they realized they were naked, tried to cover themselves, and hid from God (Genesis 3:7-8). Before, they were unclothed and lived in innocence with no flaw. After, they sensed a loss of innocence and became fearful of punishment.

The effects of their choice and Satan's are spoken when God comes to them in the Garden. One of the most moving lines in the narrative of God's story, in Genesis 3:9, is what He first said to Adam and Eve after their rebellion: "Where are you?" The yearning of His heart was fellowship and He could no longer because of humanity's willing rebellion.

Effects of their choices are set in motion by God. Satan is cursed, the original blessing to fill the earth and have dominion now has pain with it, and people physically die. In His mercy, God gives a promise of victory over the serpent. The fulfillment of this promise will result in the earth being restored (Genesis 3:15). Only God can mend the breach people created. With yearning and vision, God continued to unfold and build on this original promise in the coming generations.

Ben Melancon

Chapter 4

The Promises

"One of the most poisonous of all Satan's whispers is simply, 'Things will never change.' That lie kills expectation, trapping our heart[s]…in the present. To keep desire alive and flourishing, we must renew our vision for what lies ahead. Things will not always be like this. Jesus has promised to 'make all things new.' Eye has not seen, ear has not heard all that God has in store for his lovers, which does not mean 'we have no clue so don't even try to imagine,' but rather, you cannot out-dream God. Desire is kept alive by imagination, the antidote to resignation. We will need imagination, which is to say, we will need hope."[12]

Hope is what we have from the God of hope—by the words He has given us. He who promised is faithful and He does not lie. God created all things out of the goodness of His heart and in that inherent goodness, He provided a way to return to fellowship. Genesis 1-3 describes the wonders of creation and the disastrous effects of humanity's choice to pursue self-exaltation in exchange for dependence on God. From that time on, humanity has not known a world where there is no brokenness—tears, pain, sorrow, and death. Apart from the Scriptures telling us the end of the story, there is no portrait of what was and what is to come, and thus no hope.

Though humanity departed from fellowship with God, He undauntedly, tenaciously pursues restoration of His creation. The Bible tells the story of humanity's rebellion, and God pursuing restoration for all who come to Him. Scripture shows sin's atrocious effects and God's abundant goodness in providing a way back to fellowship. After humanity's rebellion in the beginning, a thread of God's promises runs through the remainder of Scripture from Genesis to Revelation. He promises an appointed end to this present

---

[12] Brent Curtis and John Eldredge, *The Sacred Romance: Drawing Closer to the Heart of God* (Nashville, Tennessee: Thomas Nelson, Inc., 1997).

world that is under the influence of the wicked one. Truly, there will be worldwide justice with a righteous and benevolent King who will reign forever.

The promises of restoration are fulfilled in those who accept them by faith as they seek their Maker. The one true God whose name is the Beginning and the End knows the end from beginning. "The Beginning and the End" is a name of God, as well as a time period. This title for God refers to His authority to fulfill His promises (Revelation 21:6; 22:12-13). The period of time covers "this present evil age," that started soon after creation and will end with Jesus' second coming (Galatians 1:4; Revelation 11:15). He is more than able to write His eternal love story over thousands of years through the hands of men and women who fall short of His glory. He is more than competent to fill that story with promises and keep their fulfillment within the framework of humanity's willing choice for or against Him. He is fully able to tell the story ahead of time while its fulfillment involves voluntary agreement from people.

God ties His promises' fulfillment to the few who receive His invitation to return to fellowship with Him. He tells of future events before they happen based on past promises and unfolds them with those who humble themselves, receive understanding of His plans and ways, and agree with Him in prayer for their fulfillment (John 16:13-15). We can live in vibrant expectancy that things will continue to move toward full restoration based on the promises God has made and kept. In this chapter, we will look at the thread of God's promises in the Old Testament and people who received them. These promises reveal the merciful heart of God pursuing those He made.

In agreement with Satan's logic, Adam and Eve rebelled against God's words. They sinned and death ensued. They were no longer able to fellowship with God (Romans 3:23). In the ashes of humanity's defeat, God promised to redeem them from their incurable wound of self-exaltation. In Genesis 3:15, He spoke this promise to Satan, the one who tried to subvert God's plan in the beginning:

> *And I will put enmity Between you [Satan] and the woman, And between your seed [offspring] and her Seed; He shall bruise your head, And you shall bruise His heel.*

The first promise of restoration in God's word is spoken as an eternal death blow to one who attempted to exalt himself above God. A Seed would come through Eve's descendants who would defeat Satan and be exalted over all. Here, "Seed" means offspring. In this declaration are Satan's offspring and God's offspring. God's offspring will be victorious over Satan's. Victory comes through one Seed, a son who will rule over all the earth (Revelation 12:5). This Seed would come forth in time.

Due to Adam and Eve's rebellion, humanity's hostility toward God and each other became evident as the story continued to unfold, and this involved Adam and Eve's sons, Cain and Abel. Abel pursued the Lord and received favor from Him. Cain did not seek the Lord and became jealous of his brother, leading to anger and murder. From Cain's descendants came the first recorded instance of polygamy. As evil grew, some realized their need for God and began to call on the name of the Lord (Genesis 4:26). Enoch and Noah are two who call on the Lord's name. Earth's inhabitants became so corrupt that God was going to destroy humanity completely, but Noah caught the Lord's eye as he called on His name (Genesis 6:8). Because of Noah's reach for the Lord and the Lord's reach for humanity, the earth was preserved.

With a fresh start, God gave the same blessing to Noah and His descendants that He gave to Adam and Eve: "Be fruitful and multiply, and fill the earth" (Genesis 9:1). Noah's descendants began spreading out but then rebelled against God's blessing of filling the earth. Rather than following God, they desired to make a name for themselves (Genesis 11:4). God said of them, "Indeed the people are one and they all have one language, and this is what they begin to do [build a tower to reach the heavens]; now nothing that they propose to do will be withheld from them" (Genesis 11:6). Humanity was unified in their rebellion against the Maker. To restrain their wickedness and to spread them over the earth, the Lord gave them different languages so they could no longer communicate (Genesis 11:7-9). With people spreading out across the earth, the Lord continued the thread of His promise through a man named Abram.

With Genesis 1-11 as the background, the Lord spoke three promises to Abram upon which the remainder of the Scriptures are built. These promises were also given to his son Isaac and Isaac's son, Jacob. The promises were land, a seed (offspring), and that all nations would be blessed through that seed (Genesis 12:2-3; 22:18). When the Lord first spoke with Abram, whose name was later changed to Abraham, he lived outside the land promised to him and his descendants.

The Lord shared His plan with Abraham, who lived in proximity to modern-day Iraq. God told him to go to Canaan, which is modern day Israel, and promised him:

> *²I will make you a great nation; I will bless you And make your name great; And you shall be a blessing. ³I will bless those who bless you, And I will curse him who curses you; And in you all the families of the earth shall be blessed.* (Genesis 12:2-3)

While the nations tried to made a name for themselves, the Lord told Abraham He would make Abraham's name great. He was telling Abraham the good news of His intention to bless all families of the earth through a descendant of his (Galatians 3:8). Abraham understood that this would lead to restoration of fellowship between God and people (Romans 4:1-5). The seed promised to Abraham is the eternally blessed God, through whom all the people of the earth are blessed (Romans 9:5). The Lord tells us through Paul's writing that this seed is Jesus Christ: "Now to Abraham and his Seed were the promises made. He does not say, 'And to seeds,' as of many, but as of one, '*And to your Seed,*' who is Christ" (Galatians 3:16).

The promise of a seed given to Abraham tarried. 25 years passed and in the midst of what appeared to be impossible circumstances (Sarah was around 40 years past child bearing age), the Lord fulfilled His promise and Sarah gave birth to Isaac. Through Isaac the promise of salvation for the nations marched forward (Genesis 17:19).

When Isaac was young, the Lord tested Abraham, asking him to sacrifice Isaac. This made no sense logically as it would end the promise. Reasoning that God could raise the dead, Abraham sought to obey (Hebrews 11:17-19). With knife in hand to kill Isaac, the Angel of the Lord spoke and told him not to lay a hand on his son. Because of Abraham's trust and obedience, God promised that his descendants would possess their enemies' cities, and all nations on earth would be blessed: "Then the Angel of the LORD called to Abraham a second time out of heaven, and said: 'By Myself I have sworn, says the LORD, because you have done this thing, and have not withheld your son, your only son—blessing I will bless you, and multiplying I will multiply your descendants as the stars of the heaven and as the sand which is on the seashore; and your descendants shall possess the gate of their enemies'" (Genesis 22:15-17).

Through Abraham and Isaac, the Lord tells His future story of how He will provide the way for people to be restored to relationship with Him. God gave His Son freely for the nations to return to fellowship with Him. Abraham knew that Isaac was not the complete fulfillment of the promise to bless all nations (John 8:56). The promise would come in a future generation. So he continued to act in faith, finding a wife for his son. That wife was Rebekah. She was sent off by her family with a blessing:

> *Our sister, may you become The mother of thousands of ten thousands; And may your descendants possess The gates of those who hate them.* (Genesis 24:60)

This is similar to the promise that the Angel of the Lord presented to Abraham: that his descendants would possess the gate of their enemies (Genesis 22:17).

"Possessing the gate" means having the places of authority. It equates to possessing the city. Israel possessed the physical gates of their enemies when they came out of Egypt and went into the Promised Land. However, these prophecies given to Abraham and to Rebekah have a future fulfillment as well. Abraham's natural descendants, through Isaac and Rebekah, inherited the land promised to Abraham, Isaac, and Jacob—and they will possess it forever. Abraham's spiritual descendants, the body of Christ (Romans 4:11-25), made of Jews and Gentiles from every people group, will possess the lands and cities of Jesus' enemies when He returns (Psalm 2:8; 110:2-3, 6; Revelation 2:26-27; 5:8-10). They will inherit the earth forever (Daniel 7:26-27; Matthew 5:5). Even prior to this, the gospel will prevail in every people group (Matthew 24:14), ushering in the King's return.

Following the blessing given to Rebekah, the storyline shifts its focus to Isaac's two sons, Esau and Jacob. The promises given to Abraham of land, a seed, and the nations being blessed through the seed is passed to Jacob through Isaac (Genesis 27:27-29). In this passing of the promise through generations, we see the steadfastness of God amidst humanity's fickleness.

The Lord came to Jacob in a dream and gave him the same promises He gave Abraham and Isaac. In the dream, Jacob saw a ladder resting on earth and reaching to heaven. The Lord was at the top of the ladder and angels were ascending and descending between heaven and earth (Genesis 28:12). He gave Jacob the same promise He gave to his fathers, Abraham and Isaac: "I am the LORD God of Abraham your father and the God of Isaac; the land on which you lie I will give to you and your descendants. Also your descendants shall be as the dust of the earth; you shall spread abroad to the west and the east, to the north and the south; and in you and in your seed all the families of the earth shall be blessed" (Genesis 28:13-14).

In these promises we see the descendants spreading abroad over the earth in every direction. In the Scriptures, there are physical and spiritual descendants of the promises. Physical descendants are the Jewish people. Spiritual descendants are those who receive the promises by faith as Abraham, Isaac, and Jacob did. The physical descendants of Abraham, Isaac, and Jacob have spread far and wide. Spiritual descendants, those who are of the faith of Abraham, Isaac, and Jacob, have been growing far and wide since the outpouring of the Holy Spirit after Jesus' ascension (Romans 4:11-13). They continue to grow as Jesus builds His church and truly, prior to His second coming, individuals from every people group will be blessed as they hear and receive the gospel of the kingdom, which had its beginnings in the promises made to Abraham, Isaac, and Jacob (Matthew 16:18; 24:14; Galatians 3:8).

Returning to the dream, the ladder Jacob saw connected heaven to earth and earth to heaven. The promises were given in the context of this dream. After having the dream, Jacob declared, in Genesis 28:17, "How awesome is this place! This is none other than the house of God, and this is the gate of heaven!" Jesus references this when responding to a man named Nathanael, declaring Himself to be the Son of God and King of Israel. Jesus said, "Because I said to you, 'I saw you under the fig tree,' do you believe? You will see greater things than these.' And He said to him, 'Most assuredly, I say to you, hereafter you shall see heaven open, and the angels of God ascending and descending upon the Son of Man'" (John 1:50-51). By alluding to this dream, Jesus is saying something like, "I am the Son of God, the King of Israel, and the God of Jacob. I am the seed through whom all families of the earth will be blessed. I am the house of God that will be composed of all nations. I am the gate into restored relationship with your Maker (John 2:16-21; Mark 11:17; Hebrews 3:6). I am the connecting point between heaven and earth and between the restoration of relationship between God and people." Jesus is the way into eternal fellowship with the one true God. When all peoples have heard this good news and some from each people group have received, then Jesus will return and heaven and earth will begin to be merged together (Ephesians 1:9-10; Matthew 24:14).

The dream took place in Canaan, which is modern-day Israel. The land of Israel has been promised to the Jewish people forever: the physical descendants of Abraham. As the dream shows, this is also the place where heaven and earth connect. The land of Canaan and the city of Jerusalem, located there, will be the praise of the earth and Jesus will reign from there forever (Isaiah 62:6-7; Ezekiel 43:7). Leading up to this time, the nations will militantly resist this eternal plan of God. Agreeing with the sway of Satan, they will fight for the land and the annihilation of its rightful inhabitants, and of all others who agree with God's promises (1 John 5:19).

The warfare in history and currently over the land of Israel is about who will rule the earth. This will crescendo at the end of this present age. In his attempt to rule the earth, Satan will work through a man, called the Antichrist in Scripture, attempting to take over the earth from Jerusalem and sit in the temple declaring himself to be God (2 Thessalonians 2:3-4). Jesus will defeat him and reign forever in righteousness, fulfilling the promises made to Eve, Abraham, Isaac, and Jacob (2 Thessalonians 2:8; Zechariah 14:16-19; Revelation 11:15).

In these promises given to Eve, Abraham, Isaac, and Jacob, the victory of God over Satan is certain. All the peoples of the earth will be blessed in that victory. In the promises we see that the seed is a King who will be the head of a great nation and will bring salvation to all the people groups of the earth (Genesis 12:3; 28:12-14; John 1:50-51). Many generations passed as Abraham's descendants formed the nation of Israel and came into the land of Canaan that was promised to them. The thread of God's promises then surfaced again with increased clarity to a man named David, over 1,500 years later.

Between the time of Jacob and David were several developments. Jacob and his family (the beginnings of the nation of Israel) moved from Canaan to

Egypt. Though they initially had the Egyptians' favor, eventually they went into slavery for 400 years, which the Lord spoke about ahead of time to Abraham (Genesis 15:13). At the end of these years, God brought them out of Egypt through partnership with a man named Moses. God revealed Himself to Moses as the LORD, which means "self-existent eternal One." He did not make His name, "the LORD," known to Abraham, Isaac, and Jacob (Exodus 6:3). To them, He revealed Himself as God Almighty, the One unbounded in strength and resources. To Moses, He added the name LORD, as the uncreated One who keeps His promises. He was letting Israel and Moses know that He keeps His promises made to Abraham, Isaac, and Jacob. Following their freedom from Egypt, Israel eventually took possession of the land of Canaan that was promised to Abraham, Isaac, and Jacob. Through generations of rebellion and God's patience, Israel was preserved over and over because of a few who drew near to the Lord God. God preserved them multiple times because He remembered the promises to Abraham, Isaac, and Jacob. Along the way, Israel decided they wanted a king so they could be like the peoples surrounding them. He gave them their desire and this led them further away from the Lord. While they pursued their own hearts, God pursued a man after His own heart and found one in a young shepherd boy named David (Psalm 78:70-72).

Leading up to David's kingship, the priesthood was corrupt and the nation as a whole did not seek the Lord wholeheartedly. However, a barren woman seized the Lord's attention. This woman, Hannah, longed for godly offspring in the midst of a corrupt generation. She made a vow to the Lord—if He granted her a son, she would give him to God for all the days of that son's life. The Lord gave her Samuel. She kept her vow and her son Samuel grew up in the midst of corrupt priests, while keeping himself pure. He anointed David to replace Israel's first king, Saul. Saul pursued his own heart. David, seeking God's heart, led Israel toward the Lord.

There is a parallel between Israel wanting a king according to their own heart and what will take place leading up to the Second Coming of the seed, promised throughout the Old Testament. Just as Israel desired a king rather than the Lord to rule over them, the nations will search for a leader to bring a sense of peace and safety where global turmoil looms. The Lord will give them the desire of their hearts—a man (Antichrist) who completely opposes the King of kings. During this time, the body of Christ, with the Spirit, will be in agreement for the Father to send Jesus, the eternal man after His heart to be King of the nations (Jesus is the greater David—He is the Root and the Offspring of David [Revelation 22:16-17]).

In David's time, as he received revelation of God's heart, he desired to build a dwelling place for God in Jerusalem (Psalm 132). Jerusalem is the place God desires to dwell on the earth forever in fellowship with humanity. David wrote, "For the LORD has chosen Zion; He has desired it for His dwelling place: 'This is My resting place forever; Here I will dwell, for I have desired it'" (Psalm 132:13-14). One of the first things he did after becoming Israel's king was institute continual worship to the Lord, in a tent in Jerusalem. This was the foundation of his government. He did this because he knew the Lord was the true King of Israel and that benefits of God's leadership come through partnership from His people (Psalm 22:3). Due to David's initiative, in one generation Israel went from pervasive corruption to continual worship.

After David established night and day worship, he desired to build a magnificent structure for this perpetual worship and prayer. The Lord spoke to David through the prophet Nathan about David's desire. Nathan came and told David these words from the Lord: "I took you from the sheepfold, from following the sheep, to be ruler over My people Israel. And I have been with you wherever you have gone, and have cut off all your enemies from before you, and have made you a name like the name of the great men who are on the earth. Moreover I will appoint a place for My people Israel, and will plant them, that they may dwell in a place of their own and move no more; nor shall the sons of wickedness oppress them anymore, as previously, since the time that I commanded judges to be over My people Israel. Also I will subdue all your enemies. Furthermore I tell you that the LORD will build you a house. And it shall be, when your days are fulfilled, when you must go to be with your fathers, that I will set up your seed after you, who will be of your sons; and I will establish his kingdom. He shall build Me a house, and I will establish his throne forever. I will be his Father, and he shall be My son; and I will not take My mercy away from him, as I took it from him who was before you. And I will establish him in My house and in My kingdom forever; and his throne shall be established forever" (1 Chronicles 17:7-14).

David would not build a house for the Lord. Rather, the Lord would build David a house. Solomon, David's son, went on to build a physical home for the ongoing prayer and worship, but the Lord promised David something greater than a physical house. He would build David a house by bringing forth a seed from his lineage who would establish the Lord's house and kingdom forever, on earth as it is in heaven. He will do this by reigning on David's throne, which Scripture identifies as the throne of the Lord (1 Chronicles 29:23). Jesus is that seed and will sit as a man on David's throne in Jerusalem, ruling over Israel and all nations (Isaiah 9:7; 16:5; Jeremiah 3:17; 23:5; 33:15; Luke 1:32-33; Romans 1:3; 2 Timothy 2:8; Revelation 22:16). He will be king over the whole earth (Zechariah 14:9).

This seed promised to David is the same seed promised from the beginning to Eve and to Abraham, Isaac, and Jacob. In harmony with God's storyline, the seed will crush Satan (Genesis 3:15), be the salvation of all peoples (Genesis 22:18), and rule over all the earth from Jerusalem (2 Samuel 7:12-16). God's kingdom will come fully on earth as it is in heaven and the headquarters of the kingdom will be in Jerusalem (Matthew 6:9-10; Isaiah 16:5; 62:6-7; Jeremiah 3:17). Jesus spoke much about this kingdom as He walked the earth. He said the good news of that coming kingdom will be preached in every people group on the earth, and then the end will come (Matthew 24:14). God's kingdom is a spiritual and physical kingdom, with a King who is fully God and man—Jesus Christ. He will reign forever (Isaiah 9:6-7).

After David died, Israel flourished for a generation and then moved again toward idolatry. An initial repercussion was the nation's division into the southern and northern kingdoms. As most of Israel departed from the Lord, there were a few, as in the days of old, who held to God's promises. They called the people to return to the Lord's ways. They reminded the people of God's promises and the mighty works He did in bringing them out of Egypt. The people were warned of coming judgment if they did not repent. Many Old Testament books, specifically the prophets, cover this period of time.

The prophets foretold events that took place within a couple generations while also speaking of events that would happen in the far future. The ones in the far future included Jesus' first coming, peoples from every part of the earth turning to the Lord, Jesus' second coming, Israel's complete restoration and salvation, the defeat of those who rage against God and His plans, and the bringing together of heaven and earth. These are promises rooted in the original promises of the seed made to Abraham, Isaac, Jacob, and David.

The divided kingdoms of Israel were defeated and dispersed abroad because of their willing and continual disobedience. The northern kingdom was sent into exile around 722BC by the Assyrian kingdom (2 Kings 17:6). The southern kingdom was sent into exile around 586BC by the Babylonian kingdom (2 Kings 25:1, 21). In the Lord's continual pursuit of people, there were prophets who spoke in their places of exile. One of them was Daniel.

Daniel's partnership with the Lord brought about a measure of restoration and reiterated the truth of God's coming reign over all the earth by way of the promised seed. He repented for Israel's sins and asked for God's mercy. Shortly after, due to Daniel's intercession, King Cyrus of the Persian Empire allowed the exiles to return to Israel and rebuild the place of worship. These accounts are found in Ezra, Haggai, and Zechariah. Haggai and Zechariah declared God's zeal for Jerusalem to be the praise of the earth. In agreement with Satan, the nations rage against this plan because they rage against God's leadership (Psalm 2; John 8:44). Haggai and Zechariah also reveal that God keeps His word and has all the power and resources necessary to bring about His word. The nations attempt to stand against Him. They will not succeed (Haggai 2:22; Zechariah 12:1-3; 14:1-3). Israel will be restored and Jerusalem will be the praise of the earth (Isaiah 62:5-7; 2:1-4).

The seed promised throughout the Old Testament will reign over all the earth, but not without a sacrifice. We have seen God's promises throughout the Old Testament, and those who received these promises. The promises guarantee the return to fellowship with God for all among the tribes of the earth who call on His name. Things will change. We will not always experience this present brokenness. He is faithful. By way of fellowship with God, we can stir our holy imagination through these promises and partner with the Lord, trusting Him to bring about worldwide justice and make all things new. In the next chapter, we will look at what is necessary, from God, for His promises to be fulfilled.

Ben Melancon

Chapter 5

The Lamb of God

There is an eternal King who created humanity for fellowship with Himself. Then they committed an offense that they could not right in their own strength. This led to a curse on earth and corruption of its inhabitants, bringing them below their intended vitality. A sacrifice was required for restoration of fellowship. So the King became like the inhabitants, lowering Himself into their destitution to show them the richness of His heart for them. He rescued them by becoming a sacrifice, taking all their offenses upon Himself. He was raised from the dead to never die again. All who receive Him will be raised with Him and live in eternal pleasure with Him. This is the story of God—the gospel of God's grace, who is the Maker of heaven and earth and King over all.

When we think of a king, varied images and descriptions come to mind. Probably most of these images include some form of strength and authority. This power has often been used negatively throughout the corridors of history. Strength has been wielded with pride, leading to death. Few have ruled with humility that leads to life. What is God, the great King above all kings, like? He is definitely depicted throughout Scripture with might unrivaled, owning all things, and releasing magnificent wonders that cause earth's inhabitants to tremble. Fire goes before Him, His greatness is unsearchable; He is immortal, immutable, invisible, omnipotent, eternal, and omniscient. Simultaneously, Scripture characterizes Him with lowliness and unparalleled humility, reviving the meek and strengthening those who wait on Him. His might and humility together describe His strength. Isaiah the prophet expressed both together:

For thus says the High and Lofty One who inhabits eternity, whose name is Holy: "I dwell in the high and holy place, with him who has a contrite and humble spirit, to revive the spirit of the humble, and to revive the heart of the contrite ones." (Isaiah 57:15)

God reveals his humility through becoming a man in Jesus, the seed promised to Eve, Abraham, and David. Satan rages against this humility in His pride. Through lies, Satan took the dominion of earth from God's image-bearers. God took the dominion back from Satan by offering Himself in His lovingkindness, inviting all to return to Him and have dominion with Him. Satan, depicted as a monstrous dragon, rife with evil, aimed to devour God's image-bearers. Like a lamb, Jesus was slaughtered by His image-bearers who were in agreement with Satan. With fervent zeal, God in Jesus Christ set His face like flint and offered Himself freely to bless all nations and restore the heavens and earth. The seed promised throughout the Old Testament is King of all nations from the position of being the Lamb of God who takes away the sin of the world.

After a few centuries of silence, the promised seed eventually came through David's line, but not in a way that was expected. Israel was looking for the King who would deliver them from their enemies and restore them to the "glory days" of David and Solomon. He arrived, basically unnoticed by Israel, in a barn in Bethlehem, the city of David. Jesus grew into adulthood in the same way He arrived—unnoticed, not having a physical appearance that made Him stand out (Isaiah 53:2). When the time came for Him to be revealed to Israel as the Messiah the prophets spoke of, His forerunner John the Baptist introduced Him as the Lamb of God who takes away the sin of the world (John 1:29). A lamb? Not a mighty warrior King? This was not Israel's expectation for how the kingdom would be restored to them. Rather than crushing all of Israel's enemies, their King came to be crushed by Israel and all nations.

The New Testament starts with a phrase that ties directly to the promise of the Seed threaded through the Old Testament. The New Testament's first book begins with, "The book of the genealogy of Jesus Christ, the Son of David, the Son of Abraham" (Matthew 1:1). He is the seed promised to David and Abraham who saves the Jewish people, along with all people groups, from their sin (Matthew 1:21; 1 John 2:1-2). The Lord promised Abraham that all nations would be blessed through the seed. He promised David that a

King would come through his lineage who will rule forever. He is the King through whom all nations of the earth will receive salvation.

In the Old Testament, God's sacrifice that demonstrates His goodness follows the promise of the Seed. We see the truth of humility and sacrifice from God around Adam and Eve, Abraham, and David. After Adam and Eve's rebellion and God's promise of the seed that would crush Satan, God clothed Adam and Eve with animal skins. He covered them by animal sacrifice, pointing to His own atoning sacrifice to cover sin. Later, the Lord told Abraham to sacrifice His son, the one through whom the promised seed would come. At the time of sacrifice, the Angel of the Lord came and said, "'Abraham, Abraham!' So he said, 'Here I am.' And He said, 'Do not lay your hand on the lad, or do anything to him; for now I know that you fear God, since you have not withheld your son, your only son, from Me.' Then Abraham lifted his eyes and looked, and there behind him was a ram caught in a thicket by its horns. So Abraham went and took the ram, and offered it up for a burnt offering instead of his son. And Abraham called the name of the place, The-LORD-Will-Provide; as it is said to this day, 'In the Mount of the LORD it shall be provided'" (Genesis 22:11-14). The provision of the lamb pointed to the provision of God giving His only begotten Son for the world's sins. Abraham understood that God would provide for his salvation along with all people groups. This is how all nations would be blessed in his seed. Following Abraham, David was a shepherd who became Israel's king. He saw himself as a sheep in the Lord's pasture and he understood that the Lord is the shepherd who gives Himself fully for His sheep (Psalm 23).

Isaiah depicts the seed as a humble lamb. Isaiah's name means "The LORD is salvation" and from an encounter with the LORD Almighty, he was sent as a prophet to Israel. In the encounter he saw the Lord as the King who is the Lamb slain for Israel and the nations. His message and Israel's people rejecting it revealed the hardness of their hearts toward their Maker (Isaiah 6:9-10). Isaiah's encounter marked him:

> *In the year that King Uzziah died, I saw the Lord sitting on a throne, high and lifted up, and the train of His robe filled the temple. ²Above it stood seraphim; each one had six wings: with two he covered his face, with two he covered his feet, and with two he flew. ³And one*

cried to another and said: "Holy, holy, holy is the LORD of hosts; The whole earth is full of His glory!"

⁴And the posts of the door were shaken by the voice of him who cried out, and the house was filled with smoke.

⁵So I said: "Woe is me, for I am undone! Because I am a man of unclean lips, and I dwell in the midst of a people of unclean lips; for my eyes have seen the King, The LORD of hosts."

⁶Then one of the seraphim flew to me, having in his hand a live coal which he had taken with the tongs from the altar. ⁷And he touched my mouth with it, and said: "Behold, this has touched your lips; your iniquity is taken away, and your sin purged."

⁸Also I heard the voice of the Lord, saying: "Whom shall I send, and who will go for Us?" Then I said, "Here am I! Send me." (Isaiah 6:1-8)

Isaiah tells us that he saw the LORD of hosts as King. A little more investigation reveals how he saw the King—as a lamb slain.

In this encounter, Isaiah saw Jesus, the seed promised from the beginning. He saw the LORD of hosts, the One who inhabits eternity, giving His life for the world. John 12:37-41 declares:

³⁷Although He [Jesus] had done so many signs before them, they did not believe in Him, ³⁸that the word of Isaiah the prophet might be fulfilled, which he spoke: "Lord, who has believed our report? And to whom has the arm of the LORD been revealed?"

³⁹Therefore they could not believe, because Isaiah said again: ⁴⁰"He has blinded their eyes and hardened their hearts, lest they should see with their eyes, lest they should understand with their hearts and turn, So that I should heal them."

⁴¹These things Isaiah said when he saw His glory and spoke of Him [Jesus].

John quotes Isaiah 6 and 53. The message of the two chapters are connected. Isaiah 53 depicts God's strength as a lamb slain. Isaiah prophesies from his foundational encounter in chapter 6. So Isaiah 53 is rooted in Isaiah 6. He is sent to declare God's future plan of salvation for Israel and all who call on His name. The summation of his message is that the LORD of hosts is the Holy One of Israel who is King of all nations, from the position of humbling Himself to the point of living in a human frame and giving His life freely for the world.

The nation of Israel was in rebellion against God in Isaiah's days. From the outset of his prophecies, the picture is dismal. The wound of Israel's sin is incurable and their future seems doomed as the whole nation is in rebellion (Isaiah 1:1-17). Their only hope is the redemptive nature and power of their true King. In their hopeless state, the Lord speaks through Isaiah:

> *"Come now, and let us reason together," Says the LORD, "Though your sins are like scarlet, they shall be as white as snow; though they are red like crimson, they shall be as wool."* (Isaiah 1:18)

The declaration is that He would wash away their sin in His own blood (Revelation 1:5). Later, Isaiah prophesies poignantly of Israel as sheep going astray and the Lord being slaughtered for their sins and the sins of the whole world. He says,

> *⁶All we like sheep have gone astray; we have turned, every one, to his own way; and the LORD has laid on Him the iniquity of us all. He was oppressed and He was afflicted, yet He opened not His mouth; ⁷He was led as a lamb to the slaughter, and as a sheep before its shearers is silent, so He opened not His mouth.* (Isaiah 53:6-7)

He did this to "sprinkle many nations" (Isaiah 52:15). The depiction of God as a lamb slaughtered for the sins of Israel and all peoples pointed Israel to the centerpiece of their nation. Israel came into a covenant with the one true God (Exodus 19:3-8). They approached Him by way of a sacrificial system where sheep and cows were killed to atone for the people's sin. Throughout their history, these sacrifices became rituals without repentant hearts that stood in awe of God's kindness. This was the case in Isaiah's day.

When Isaiah saw the Lord Almighty high and lifted up, it evoked a major response in him. In Isaiah 6:5, he cried out,

Woe is me, for I am undone! Because I am a man of unclean lips, and I dwell in the midst of a people of unclean lips; for my eyes have seen the King, the LORD of hosts.

What did Isaiah see to evoke that reaction? After his response, a seraph touched his lips with a burning coal from the altar and declared, "Your iniquity is taken away, and your sin purged" (Isaiah 6:7). The altar points to animal sacrifice or incense. Either way, both were necessary in approaching the Holy of Holies, where God's glory dwelt. Isaiah is cleansed by a coal from under the altar so he can prophesy to Israel and the nations. I imagine Isaiah coming out of the encounter saying something like, "If the people I live among could see Israel's king: how great, how humble, and how committed He is to them–if they could see the true King, the Holy One of Israel as the Lamb slain who is our eternal High Priest, they would turn and be healed as I have been. They do not comprehend the significance of these daily sacrifices. They do not see in them their own King and High Priest being sacrificed on the altar for them."

From this encounter, Isaiah became a messenger of comfort for Israel and all among humanity who call on His name. Before the Babylonians scattered Israel's southern kingdom among the nations, Isaiah prophesied comfort to Israel (Isaiah 40:1-2; 40-66). He spoke of Israel's eventual full restoration and of all humanity seeing the Lord's glory (return of Jesus). Condensed, his message of comfort concerning the restoration of Jerusalem reads:

⁶The voice said, "Cry out!" And he said, "What shall I cry?" "All flesh is grass, and all its loveliness is like the flower of the field. ⁷The grass withers, the flower fades, because the breath of the LORD blows upon it; surely the people are grass. ⁸The grass withers, the flower fades but the word of our God stands forever." (Isaiah 40:6-8)

The message is that the entirety of humanity's labor is futile when not done in fellowship with their Maker. Because of this truth, the call for Israel and all nations is to receive the Lord as the Good Shepherd who lays down His life for the world's sin (Isaiah 40:11; 45:21-23). He is able and will save Israel along with all from the peoples of the earth who put their trust in Him (Isaiah

40:27-31), and He will reign from Jerusalem forever in a new heavens and new earth.

As Isaiah was a voice of comfort sent by the Lord Almighty, he prophesied of another messenger who would prepare the way for Jesus' first coming, John the Baptist (Isaiah 40:3). He further spoke of many who prepare the way for His second coming:

> *"Comfort, yes, comfort My people!" Says your God. ²"Speak comfort to Jerusalem, and cry out to her, That her warfare is ended, That her iniquity is pardoned; For she has received from the LORD's hand Double for all her sins." ³The voice of one crying in the wilderness: "Prepare the way of the LORD; Make straight in the desert A highway for our God. ⁴Every valley shall be exalted And every mountain and hill brought low; The crooked places shall be made straight And the rough places smooth; ⁵The glory of the LORD shall be revealed, And all flesh shall see it together; For the mouth of the LORD has spoken."* (Isaiah 40:1-5)

The Lord's glory was not revealed to all people in John the Baptist's day. We know that it will be at Jesus' return (Revelation 1:7). Thus, Isaiah was speaking of a people who were yet to come who would prepare the way for His second coming. They do this by declaring the gospel of the kingdom to every people group—the gospel of the coming King who became the Lamb slain for the world's sins. They do this from having a revelation of the Lamb slain as Isaiah did. The church has done this since its inception, but there will be a final generation where it will be proclaimed like never before in history.

Like Isaiah, John the apostle saw Jesus as the Lamb slain and was given more insight. Both saw the One with supreme authority, yet slaughtered like a sin offering lamb. Isaiah was distraught as he saw his own state in the presence of God's holiness. John was undone, weeping at the thought of no one being capable to fix the world in its present state of injustice. The Isaiah 6 and Revelation 5 accounts are similar. We will look at Revelation in detail in a later chapter. Here I will summarize Revelation, and we will look briefly at chapter 5.

The book of Revelation displays Jesus as the Lamb slain and resurrected as the Anointed Savior and King (Revelation 5:5-6). At His second coming,

He will defeat all who are proud and lofty among the raging nations, along with what they "accomplished" apart from Him (Isaiah 2; 40:1-8). He does this because of their seething hatred for and their open rejection of His love displayed for them on the cross. As the Lamb slain, Jesus became High Priest forever for all who call upon His name (Revelation 1:13; 5:6). To this present moment He lives to make intercession for all who come to God through Him (Hebrews 7:25). His sacrifice is so generous and His intercession so effective that members of every people group will stand before Him in heaven declaring: "Salvation belongs to our God who sits on the throne, and to the Lamb!" (Revelation 7:10). Simultaneously, people from across the earth will reject and openly rage against Him (Revelation 13:3-4; Mathew 24:9).

Revelation 5 showcases the worthiness of Jesus to rule the nations in righteousness. The One who sits on the throne has a scroll in His right hand and the question rings out from a strong angel, "Who is worthy to open the scroll and to loose its seals?" (Revelation 5:2). In other words, "Who can lead the nations in everlasting righteousness and right all of the injustice that has ravaged the earth since Adam and Eve's rebellion?" No one is worthy in the entirety of heaven and earth, except One. An elder instructs John to behold the worthy One, calling Him the Lion of the tribe of Judah and the Root of David (Revelation 5:5). John turns his attention to this Lion of Judah and sees a lamb as though it had been slain (Revelation 5:6).

Like Isaiah, John saw the King of all kings offering His strength by way of humility. The "Lion of the Tribe of Judah" and the "Root of David" are kingly titles. This aligns with the Old Testament prophecies that a king would rise from David's line who will lead Israel and the nations into everlasting righteousness (Jeremiah 23:5-6). "Lion of Judah" is a prophecy from Jacob about Jesus (Genesis 49:8-11). He comes from Judah's lineage and "to Him shall be the obedience of the people" (Genesis 49:10). "Root of David" is from Isaiah 11: "There shall come forth a Rod from the stem [root] of Jesse, and a Branch shall grow out of his roots." (Isaiah 11:1). Jesse is David's father, the physical root of David. David is promised a descendant who will rule forever. Jesus existed before David as the Lord, but was birthed through his lineage as a human to save the world from its sin. The Root of David coming forth will result in the restoration of the earth to God's original purposes (Isaiah 11). By way of the King giving Himself for all peoples, He is exalted to the highest place and those who receive Him will eternally reign with Him (Philippians 2:5-11; Revelation 5:8-10).

Jesus Christ, the seed promised throughout God's story, gave His life because of His yearning for His image-bearers to return to fellowship with Him. When Isaiah saw Jesus' glory, he heard the declaration, "Holy, holy, holy is the LORD of hosts; The whole earth is full of His glory!" (Isaiah 6:3). The whole earth is full of people made in His image, in His glory (Genesis 1:26-27; Isaiah 42:8; 43:7, 21). He is zealous to have His own; not only Israel is filled with His glory, but all the world. Isaiah also prophesied of Jesus as the One who brings justice to the whole earth by giving His life for the world (Isaiah 42:1-4; Hebrews 9:14). He gives His life for His glory among the nations. His glory is not just that His image-bearers worship Him forever. His glory is the delight of His goodness that He gets to bestow forever on those who receive Him, and them expressing gratitude as they bask in His eternal pleasures.

In this chapter, we observed God's humility paralleling His promises of the seed to restore fellowship with His image-bearers. The seed spoken of throughout the Old Testament is indeed King of the nations, but from the position of being the Lamb of God slain for the world's sins. This seed has now been revealed in Christ who was sacrificed. He was raised from the dead and is now sitting at the right hand of the Father, forever victorious over death and possessing all authority in heaven and on earth (Revelation 1:17-18; Matthew 28:18). Before going to the Father's right hand, He gave a command to propagate what He started in Israel, proceeding to the ends of the earth, ushering in the restoration of fellowship with humanity among all peoples. In Part 2 we will peer into the fulfillment of God's promises in Christ and how we partner with Him to complete what He started.

Ben Melancon

Part 2
God's Commission

Chapter 6

The Call to Go

For several years, I have been part of a weekly gathering that prepares the way for the King's second coming. This takes place on Wednesday mornings at the International House of Prayer in Atlanta, Georgia. For two hours the worship and prayer team, with those who come to participate, join in worship and intercession for the fulfillment of Jesus' Great Commission (Matthew 28:18-20). At one of these meetings, we were praying for Bible translation projects around the world, asking the Lord for laborers according to Matthew 9:36-38. After one particular prayer, a team singer began repeating, "How can they hear unless we go?" The word "go" struck me, and Matthew 28:19 came to mind: "Go therefore and make disciples of all the nations." As we pray according to Jesus' directive, adding to every prayer since the church's inception for the mission's fulfillment, laborers are going forth, accomplishing God's mission with Him.

A couple of days after this prayer meeting I watched *Better Friends than Mountains*, a documentary about people groups in Northern Iraq. It highlighted the importance of going, as Jesus commanded. As I saw the Kurdish people and the Yazidi people, the call to go to every people group became clearer. Laborers among these peoples expressed that the need is for workers to come and live the love of God. Entire groups of people, some small and some large, exist without a gospel witness and have no access to the truth of God's love. Yet, Jesus gave a command to go, promising the proclamation of the gospel to every people group on earth (Matthew 24:14).

Jesus gave those who knew Him a mission to accomplish with Him. The purpose of the mission is to finish what He started. He began the spread of the good news and made its continuation possible through giving the Holy Spirit to those who believe. The message continues to spread to this present day through people who have received the extravagant mercy of the King of kings and Lord of lords. The mission's completion will result in individuals from each people group walking in restored fellowship with God, fulfilling God's original promise of blessing to Abraham's seed among all nations.

He gave the mission to His disciples following His resurrection. Victorious over sin and death, Jesus met His apostles and gave them the mission: "All authority has been given to Me in heaven and on earth. Go therefore and make disciples of all the nations, baptizing them in the name of the Father and of the Son and of the Holy Spirit, teaching them to observe all things that I have commanded you; and lo, I am with you always, even to the end of the age" (Matthew 28:18-20).

The mission Jesus gave denotes His authority, the church's partnership with Him, and the assurance of His presence that comforts them as they fulfill the mission. Many call Jesus' command to go to all the earth's peoples with the gospel the "Great Commission." A "commission" entrusts others with power and sends them on a mission. As the body of Christ, we are to put our confidence in Jesus' authority and go with Him to all peoples to share the gospel with them and disciple them.

Jesus' statement of His supreme authority in heaven and on earth tells us that victory is certain. Through the cross, He disarmed all principalities and powers that stand against Him. He has the name that all must kneel to, and all must confess that He is truly the LORD of the Old Testament (Isaiah 45:21-23; Philippians 2:9-11). There is no other God. He now has authority in heaven and earth *as a man*. He received this authority by conquering the sin and death resulting from Adam and Eve's rebellion against God. Paul referenced this victory when writing to his spiritual son Timothy: "[God] has saved us and called us with a holy calling, not according to our works, but according to His own purpose and grace which was given to us in Christ Jesus before time began, but has now been revealed by the appearing of our Savior Jesus Christ, who has abolished death and brought life and immortality to light through the gospel" (2 Timothy 1:9-10). He is now alive forever at the Father's right hand, holding the keys of death (Hebrews 1:3; Revelation 1:18).

When Jesus died on the cross and rose from the dead, He received spiritual and physical dominion as a man. A few weeks later, He ascended to the Father's right hand and poured out His Spirit on His disciples and a few others, releasing His spiritual dominion in them. From there, they began proclaiming the gospel in Israel and to the ends of the earth. Many from various people groups received the message and began walking in spiritual dominion over bondage to sin and the fear of death. However, physical dominion over all of God's enemies, the saints obtaining immortal bodies, and the restoration of the heavens and earth, has not yet happened. Satan still has sway over the earth, in physical and spiritual dominion over those who reject Jesus.

With the church operating in spiritual dominion, Jesus sits at the Father's right hand and waits for His enemies to become His footstool—waiting for physical dominion. Hebrews articulates, "[T]his Man, after He had offered one sacrifice for sins forever, sat down at the right hand of God, from that time waiting till His enemies are made His footstool" (Hebrews 10:12-13). Waiting for His enemies to become His footstool alludes to Psalm 110, the most quoted scripture from the Old Testament in the New Testament. In this Psalm, David had a revelation of the heavenly coronation of Jesus as King who sits down and waits for His enemies to become His footstool. What does He await and how is the Father putting His enemies under His feet? He waits for the proclamation of the gospel to every people group, by the Spirit, through people who have come to know Him. As this happens, His spiritual power is made known to principalities and powers in the heavenly realms, through how the church expresses itself in meekness that comes from God's wisdom (Ephesians 1:17-22; 3:10-12). When the final people group hears and some receive, events will be set in motion for Jesus to come and take physical dominion of the earth as people from each people group welcome Him back. The first half of Psalm 110 shows His spiritual dominion; the second half depicts His physical dominion.

Having supreme authority, Jesus calls those who know Him to go and do what He did in Israel. We are to make followers of Jesus, who abide in Him and walk in humble obedience. We do not make followers of people, a denomination, or a list of rules. We make followers of the man Christ Jesus and teach them to abide in His love. From there, they will grow in love and fulfill God's will as He directs their paths. The call to be part of the Great Commission is to all believers because we are all in God's family, through Jesus Christ, and this is His mission He left us to accomplish with Him. We may not all go to unreached peoples, but we all play a part, as discussed in Part 3 of this book. However, to accomplish the mission, some must and will go.

Missions strategy should be "ready, aim, fire," not "ready, aim, aim, aim." There are various reasons for aiming and not firing. Regardless of what they are and knowing that there is wisdom in waiting for the Lord's timing, there comes a time when we must fire. We must go out as laborers to unreached areas. Plans and strategies can be good, if we implement them. In our implementation, we go in the reality that not everything will be according to our plans and strategies. This keeps us dependent on the Lord of the harvest to do His work in His way. We do not fulfill the mission from a driving sense of duty, but as friends who abide in the love of the Savior and Harvest Chief. In physical war, plans and strategies help us prepare, but when battle breaks out, things often do not go according to our expectations. In the spiritual war of delivering people from the kingdom of darkness, we go with plans and strategies God has given us as we depend on Him to guide us through the battlefield in the midst of our enemies. We fix our eyes on the Commander and Chief who is ever with us and in us.

The Commander and Chief, Jesus, gives us all we need to accomplish His mission because He gives us Himself. In Him, we have all we need internally for the mission and He will provide all external resources along the journey. All of creation, including all the gold and silver, is His. Knowing this, we can gladly go wherever He leads. He provides all necessary provision and tools in every context. He is the Harvest Chief. He has all the credentials to lead the mission and all the grace needed for us to walk in Him and see the mission fulfilled.

The Lord of the harvest is not telling us to fulfill His mission for Him. After speaking of His supreme authority and giving the command to go, Jesus said, "I am with you always, even to the end of the age" (Matthew 28:20). He chose us to abide in His love and from there to accomplish His mission with Him. When preparing His disciples for the coming mission, He assured them that they were not the ones who came up with the idea of following Him, but He chose them, and they were to simply enjoy being in Him. The mission starts and finishes through this fellowship. He said, "You did not choose Me, but I chose you and appointed you that you should go and bear fruit, and that your fruit should remain, that whatever you ask the Father in My name He may give you" (John 15:16). The pressure is off of us to fulfill the mission in our own strength. We go and make disciples through being in Jesus, living joyfully dependent on Him, and the fruit of disciple making is certain to manifest (John 15:5, 9, 16). God's kingdom will grow and eventually become the largest plant in the garden of the earth (Matthew 13:31-32).

The assurance of Jesus being with us settles reservations. Only God has the power to never leave us nor forsake us on a physical, emotional, and spiritual level. None but Jesus can make this promise and has the power to keep it. One of the most troubling things to the human heart is the fear of being alone. Jesus addressed this, telling us that He will give us His peace and make His home in us (John 14:15-27). He promises He will be with us to the end of the age and will raise us up at the last day. As we go with Him, He confirms His word that we speak.

We can trust Jesus to release His authority in and through us as we tell all peoples about Him. God confirms the good news of His kingdom by signs, wonders, various miracles, and gifts of the Holy Spirit, distributed according to His will (Hebrews 2:4). Jesus said this would happen: "Go into all the world and preach the gospel to every creature. He who believes and is baptized will be saved; but he who does not believe will be condemned. And these signs will follow those who believe: In My name they will cast out demons; they will speak with new tongues; they will take up serpents; and if they drink anything deadly, it will by no means hurt them; they will lay hands on the sick, and they will recover" (Mark 16:15-18). We are to anticipate and expect things beyond our own ability when we preach the gospel. Why would we not believe for all God wants to do? We miss part of God's heart and power when we do not anticipate these things. He wants to save people while demonstrating the power of the kingdom of light that heals and sets people free physically and emotionally, not just spiritually. When signs and wonders accompany the gospel message, it is a manifestation of Jesus' victory over Satan. Jesus spoke of this after sending laborers on a mission to declare His coming kingdom. They came back and reported what they experienced. Jesus responded, "I saw Satan fall like lightning from heaven" (Luke 10:18). These people had declared the kingdom, healed the sick, and driven out demons in Jesus' name. Through this, Jesus demonstrated the power He has over Satan, and his coming demise when He returns. We are to go in the same way—preaching the gospel, teaching the kingdom, and trusting God to confirm it with signs and wonders.

This template given in Luke 10 is a pattern the church is to follow with Jesus to the ends of the earth. After saying that He saw Satan fall like lightning from heaven, Jesus went on to proclaim, "Behold, I give you the authority to trample on serpents and scorpions, and over all the power of the enemy, and nothing shall by any means hurt you" (Luke 10:19). Jesus said miracles would accompany believers, as we ask (John 14:12-13). However, we do not rejoice that demons are subject to us or that people are healed, but that our names are written in heaven (Luke 10:20)! We enjoy the journey with Jesus and trust Him to reveal Himself in extraordinary ways among all peoples, just as He did among the Jews.

We follow the Harvest Chief, who has all the plans for the how and when of the harvest. This involves times of training and waiting. In agriculture, for a field's harvest, there is work that is done to make the harvest possible. There is waiting for the right time. In the spiritual realm, Jesus knows where all the people groups, who He identifies as fields, are located (Matthew 13:38). He also knows how, when, and through who the harvest will come in. Jesus spent the first 30 years of His life waiting and growing in fellowship with the Father. When the time came, He was sent in the Spirit's power (Luke 4:14, 18-19). Even when sent, Jesus lived a lifestyle of "waiting"— abiding in the Father's love through the Spirit and doing as He saw His Father doing. He tells us to live the same way (John 5:19-20; 15:5, 9, 15). Before He sent His disciples to disciple the nations, He told them to wait for the Spirit's power and sending (Luke 24:49; Acts 1:8). Paul and Barnabas were in a time of fasting and prayer (waiting) when the Lord called them to unreached people groups (Acts 13:2-3). At present, the Harvest Chief is training and sending laborers to the earth's last remaining fields. He will give us His power and resources as we abide in Him. We can discern when to pray and fast, waiting to be endued with power for the specific mission before us.

Jesus began a mission that will have a global effect. He started the mission that fulfills the Old Testament promise to bless all nations through Abraham's seed. He continues that mission through His church. He has all authority over the bondage of sin and fear of death, and He is always with us. He requires us to abide in His love, listen for His voice, and go as He directs. He calls us to go by His own example and promises to be with us. The next chapter explains Jesus' intentional focus of having all nations as

Chapter 7

To the Ends of the Earth

"Are you a king?" asked Pilate, as he questioned Jesus about why He was arrested. Jesus answered, "You say rightly that I am a king. For this cause I was born, and for this cause I have come into the world, that I should bear witness to the truth. Everyone who is of the truth hears My voice" (John 18:37). Jesus came into the world to bear witness to the truth of His love that conquers sin and destroys Satan's works (1 John 3:6, 8). Jesus is the truth who sets people free from bondage to sin. He is the king whose kingdom is not of this world, and this kingdom will overtake the present world that is under the evil one's sway (Revelation 11:15). The Old Testament speaks much about the LORD being King of all. Jesus is that LORD and King. In Jesus the King, God the Father delivers us from the kingdom of darkness, bringing us into the kingdom of light.

The Lord put on flesh, coming through a human womb. He is returning in flesh at His second coming, riding on the clouds, and He will set up His throne on earth. In mercy, Jesus gave His life for the world, providing salvation to all who call upon His name among the Jews and Gentiles (Romans 11:32). Some from every people group on earth will receive Him while many will rage against Him. He is returning by invitation from His church He builds, made of people from every tribe. For this to happen, His church must be fully built.

For Jesus' church to be fully built, the gospel must proceed through flesh and blood filled with the Holy Spirit. As water bubbles from a spring out of the depths of the earth, so God's gospel, encapsulated by different skin colors and cultures, flows across the globe. When complete, the kingdom of this world will be given over to Jesus and He will reign forever with His people (Daniel 7:13-14, 18). He has given His church the honor of agreeing with His desire for every tribe, through intercession and through proclaiming the gospel to the ends of the earth with Him. He gave us a template for doing so, by His own example and by giving us a snapshot of how His first disciples walked this out.

Jesus came to earth the first time in fulfillment of many Old Testament prophecies, opening the way for other prophecies to be fulfilled leading up to His second coming. As an example, He had to be rejected by people, crucified, and raised from the dead, thus providing the way for the ends of the earth to turn to Him, to righteously judge the world, and to set up His kingdom on earth as in heaven at His second coming (Psalm 22:27; Isaiah 53:8-12). The gospel accounts of Matthew and John reveal Jesus' global focus and the pattern for how the message of the kingdom progresses to the ends of the earth. The places Jesus traveled to, who He ministered to, and miracles that followed His teaching and preaching are given to us as a blueprint for how God desires the message of the kingdom to be globally propagated. Like a master craftsman intentionally guides his apprentices so that the craft may continue into future generations, so the Spirit testifies of a clear pattern in Scripture, teaches us the pathway, and empowers us to propagate the message. The book of Acts shows how Jesus' disciples followed this pattern under the Holy Spirit's leadership. Jesus gives the blueprint, and in Acts, the first disciples walk out this blueprint.

In Matthew, the Holy Spirit emphasizes the kingdom of heaven, Jesus as the King, the values of the kingdom, and the certainty of its coming on earth as in heaven. The book begins by declaring Jesus Christ as the son of David and the son of Abraham. He is the One promised to David who will be King forever. He is the One promised to Abraham through whom all nations have salvation. Many of the parables focus on the kingdom of heaven and many of the prophecies mentioned from the Old Testament point to Jesus as King of that kingdom. Jesus states the values of the kingdom and speaks in parables of the spread of this kingdom and the certainty of its prevailing. Like leaven that works its way through every part of bread dough, so God's kingdom will spread to every tribe on earth. The book ends with Jesus commissioning His disciples to finish with Him what He started, spreading the message of the kingdom and its effects to all peoples.

From the start of his gospel account, Matthew focuses on identifying Jesus as King as he cites Old Testament prophecies. The time came for the promised seed to spring from Mary. As a virgin, through the Spirit, she brought forth a

Son whose name means "Savior" and who will rule all nations (Revelation 12:5). Isaiah spoke of Him as Immanuel, meaning "God with us" (Isaiah 7:14; Matthew 1:23). He is from everlasting and will reign forever (Matthew 2:6; Micah 5:2; Revelation 11:15).

Over time, the King grew into a young man and another man began to prepare the way for Him to be revealed to Israel. This preparer's name was John and he called people to repent because the kingdom of heaven was at hand. He is known as John the Baptist because he baptized those who responded with repentance. The kingdom was close because the King was present. One day while John was baptizing, Jesus came to be baptized, though He was sinless. By doing this He humbled Himself and pointed to the cross where He would bear the world's sins. He made a statement of His commitment to fulfill the righteousness of God, giving His life freely, inviting all peoples to receive His righteousness (Matthew 3:15; Romans 3:25-26).

Both validation and testing followed this willing act and His statement that He would fulfill all righteousness. At Jesus' baptism, an audible voice from heaven declared, "This is My beloved Son, in whom I am well pleased" (Matthew 3:17). This shows the Lord as the Father delighting over His son, and points back to David's prophecy from Psalm 2, indicating He will have all nations as His inheritance (Psalm 2:7-8). Following this, the devil tested Him with the invitation to worship him in exchange for the kingdoms of the world (Matthew 4:8-9). This shows that the devil knew Jesus had come to destroy his works and take the kingdom of this world from him, not by worshipping him but by crushing his head through humble dependency on His Father. Standing successfully against the kingdom of darkness, the King began to manifest the presence of His kingdom. He did this by preaching, teaching, and healing rather than killing, stealing, and destroying (Matthew 4:23-25; John 10:10). He became well known among the Jewish people, and among predominantly Gentile lands.

In the midst of this renown, Jesus taught His disciples the values of His eternal kingdom (Matthew 5-7). He trained them in the values of His kingdom so they could train nations (Matthew 28:18-20). I imagine Jesus saying something like, "The dream of My heart, My worth, and My success is not being popular and known for physical healing. That is not the main point of My kingdom, nor is it My source of satisfaction. I will tell you the way to true joy and success: I long for people's hearts. I want to transform you into my nature so you can reign with Me forever. I desire this to be true of you along with people from every tribe across the earth."

Jesus unashamedly explains the values of God's kingdom and how they are the way to true blessing. He gives values that are the opposite of the nations' ways, and calls His disciples to seek first His kingdom and righteousness (Matthew 5:3-13; 6:33). Walking in these values is what Jesus considers true discipleship. He embodies them perfectly. They are His nature. Mercy is His nature. Meekness is His nature. He tells us that living in His values is the way to greatness in His kingdom (Matthew 5:19), how we walk as children of our Father (Matthew 5:43-48), what we are to seek first (Matthew 6:33), how we walk the narrow way (Matthew 7:13-14), and how we build our life on the rock, on Him, not on the sand of our own righteousness (Matthew 7:24-25).

After expressing His values, the story continues, showing effects of Jesus' preaching, teaching, and healing while intentionally focusing on His mission to have all nations as His inheritance (Matthew 8-9). Just prior to stating His values, He had become known to Jews and Gentiles and had probably even healed some Gentiles (Matthew 4:23). After stating the values, a Gentile asks Jesus to heal one of his servants. Amazed at the Gentile's faith, Jesus says, "Assuredly, I say to you, I have not found such great faith, not even in Israel! And I say to you that many will come from east and west, and sit down with Abraham, Isaac, and Jacob in the kingdom of heaven" (Matthew 8:10-11). He paints a picture of a global gathering for His marriage supper (Revelation 19:6-7). As He continues to labor, He lifts His eyes to see multitudes, is moved with compassion, and invites His disciples to pray to the Lord of the harvest to send laborers into His harvest (Matthew 9:36-38).

Jesus gave us His leadership model for how to make disciples, reaching to the ends of the earth. He prioritizes focusing on the principles He embodied in humble dependency on His Father. He trained His disciples and He trains us in His kingdom's values, teaching us to pray for the spread of these values (Matthew 4:23-7:27; 9:35-38). Laborers preach the message of the kingdom, teach the values that are transforming them by Christ, and heal in testifying of the goodness of God's kingdom and the power of the coming age. Jesus looks for laborers who invite Him to work His values into them. Filled with His values, they are filled with His dream for His values to go to every tribe. So they ask the Lord of the harvest to send out laborers who spread His values in word and deed to every people.

With the template set by His own example, Jesus gives a foretaste of what will happen to the ends of the earth. He does this by anointing His original 12 disciples to go out, preaching the kingdom and healing (Matthew 10:1, 7-8). He speaks of fierce resistance to the spread of the kingdom message and its power (Matthew 10-11). Then He tells a few parables that describe the absolute certainty of His kingdom's expansion until it fills all the earth (Matthew 13:1-52). Following His resurrection, this expansion went beyond Israel's borders and has been victoriously expanding since that time.

This expansion takes place based on the truth of Christ's identity. After feeding a great multitude through multiplying bread and fish, which speaks of multiplication of God's kingdom through Jesus' death and resurrection (John 6), He asks His disciples a question foundational to releasing His kingdom: "'Who do men say that I, the Son of Man, am?' So they said, 'Some say John the Baptist, some Elijah, and others Jeremiah or one of the prophets.' He said to them, 'But who do you say that I am?' Simon Peter answered and said, 'You are the Christ, the Son of the living God.' Jesus answered and said to him, 'Blessed are you, Simon Bar-Jonah, for flesh and blood has not revealed this to you, but My Father who is in heaven. And I also say to you that you are Peter, and on this rock I will build My church, and the gates of Hades shall not prevail against it. And I will give you the keys of the kingdom of heaven, and whatever you bind on earth will be bound in heaven, and whatever you loose on earth will be loosed in heaven'" (Matthew 16:13-19).

Jesus spoke this in a place called Caesarea Philippi, a crossroad of cultures of the Canaanites, Greeks, and Romans, who gave themselves to idolatry. Following is a brief historical account, "Caesarea Philippi was the location [of] the Cave of Pan, the place of the pagan Gate of Hades. It was in this area that the first king of Israel (Jeroboam) led the northern kingdom of Israel into idolatry. This was also the same place where the Greeks and Romans received revelations from the god Pan who was mentioned in classical writings as a 'seer' or fortune teller and a giver of revelations."[13] At this very spot, a

---

[13] "Ancient Caesarea Philippi," Bible History Online, http://www.bible-history.com/biblestudy/caesarea-philippi.html.

revelation is given to Peter that Jesus is the Anointed One who is the Son of the living God. On the rock of revelation of who He is, His church is being built among all tribes, to turn them from Satan's power to the power of God (Acts 26:17-18). The gates of Hades, nor effects of the reign of sin and death, can prevail against God's zeal to bring the nations into fellowship with Himself.

After this conversation, Jesus began to periodically mention His coming death and resurrection. He resolutely set out to Jerusalem to freely give His life for the world (Matthew 21-23). Keeping in focus Jesus as King, Matthew recounts Jesus riding into Jerusalem on a donkey, fulfilling a prophecy from Zechariah about the coming King (Zechariah 9:9). Following this came a week of outright resistance to Jesus from Jewish leadership. During this time, He declares Himself to be the Anointed One (Christ - King) from Psalm 110 and rebukes the hypocritical Jewish leadership (Matthew 22:42-45; 23).

Walking away from the center of Jerusalem, Jesus answers a question His disciples asked concerning His reign. They want to know what will be the sign of the end of the age and His return as King, that He had spoken about in some parables. They want to know when the kingdom will be restored to Israel (Acts 1:6). He outlines events that will take place in the generation of His return and declares that the end will not come until the gospel has been declared as a witness to all peoples (Matthew 24:14). Then is a time of great tribulation the world has never seen nor will see again (Matthew 24:21). After this tribulation, Jesus will return, completing God's plan (Matthew 24:29-31; Revelation 10:7; 11:15). Jesus gave His church details on how to prepare for this time and usher in Jesus' coming and kingdom. He does this by telling three parables (Matthew 24:45-25:30). The parables speak of being faithful to prepare others, lifestyles that prioritize intimacy with God through prayer, and faithfulness with resources He gives to spread the gospel until it reaches every people.

To make the spread of the kingdom possible, Jesus destroyed the devil's work through the cross (Matthew 26-27). He accomplished this by giving His life and resurrecting three days later (Matthew 28:1-7). He appeared to His disciples and others, releasing the mission that will result in people from every tribe becoming His inheritance (Matthew 28:18-20). The mission will be finished by God's own zeal, through human agents who have received His

Spirit. The mission is not merely a task to fulfill with the Father, Son, and Holy Spirit, but flows from a burning fellowship to show the King's heart to every people, and invite them into union with Him forevermore. The gospel of John depicts this.

We will look at John by observing two main paradigms the Holy Spirit emphasizes. One is Jesus' relationship with His Father and the other is inviting the nations into the same relationship. Throughout the book of John, Jesus speaks much and highly of His Father—of the love the Father has for Jesus and for the entire world, created through Jesus. Because of this love, Jesus came to invite people into the rich, eternal relationship He experiences with His Father. Speaking to Mary Magdalene after His resurrection, Jesus says, "Do not cling to Me, for I have not yet ascended to My Father; but go to My brethren and say to them, 'I am ascending to My Father and your Father, and to My God and your God'" (John 20:17). Jesus says to Mary, "My Father is your Father. My God is your God"! Jesus tells Mary she has the same relationship with the Father that He has. Jesus invites us all into this relationship (John 14:16-17). This is like a lowly servant being upgraded to the same relationship as a wealthy family's firstborn son. We are invited to be co-heirs with the appointed heir of all things (Romans 8:17; Hebrews 1:2). The first half of John focuses heavily on the relationship between Jesus and His Father, and the second half focuses more on the relationship available to all who call upon His name, though these truths are intertwined throughout.

Jesus emphasized two ways He represented the Father as He walked the earth. He spoke the Father's words and did the Father's works. Looking at them together, the words and works testify of God's nature, and His plans to give all nations to Jesus as His inheritance, because of His nature (John 4:34; 5:17, 36, 12:48-50; 14:10, 24; 17:4). The Father gives the nations to Jesus as His inheritance, through those who have received Him, are transformed by Him, and go with Him by the Spirit to the ends of the earth. Abiding in the same relationship Jesus had with the Father, the church's focus is testifying of Jesus and His relationship with the Father, and inviting all peoples into this relationship.

The gospel of John begins and ends with the *whole* world in view. At the beginning John wrote, "He was in the world, and the world was made through Him, and the world did not know Him. He came to His own, and His own did not receive Him. But as many as received Him, to them He gave the right to become children of God, to those who believe in His name" (John 1:10-12). At the end of the book, John quotes Jesus' words, "Peace to you! As the Father has sent Me, I also send you [into the world]" (John 20:21b). Jesus came into the world, testified of the Father's desire to give eternal life to all who receive Him, and sent His disciples into the world to declare the message until all peoples hear (John 17:1-3,18; Matthew 24:14). The contents between are congruent with the book's beginning and end.

The eternal relationship from which creation came forth is how John starts his gospel account. Just as an artist strategically brushes each stroke to bring forth a picture, so brush strokes are utilized here, forming a picture that describes the reason for humanity's existence. All of creation came through what John called the "Word." This Word was with God, was God, and all creation came through Him. He is life and is light for humanity. He was with God and yet is God (John 1:1-4). This depiction provides an opening into the vast mystery of the relationship of God operating among Himself as Father, Son, and Holy Spirit. We can peer into the burning desire that produced creation and marvel at God valuing the human spirit so much that He formed man in His own image. Meditating on this shows us eternal purpose behind our existence.

A little later in John, more is given to describe the Word of God. The Word who was with God in the beginning and who made all things became flesh, and His name is Jesus Christ. He came into the world to reveal God's grace and truth, and to invite us into the eternal experience of being filled with that grace and truth. He came to invite us into our true identity as God's children who are in His family forever (John 1:12). He became flesh to fulfill the promise given to Abraham, Isaac, and Jacob—that through them a seed (offspring) would rise to bless all peoples. Jesus is identified as that seed, highlighting the promise given to Jacob (John 1:51; Galatians 3:16). He is the One through whom all things in heaven and earth are brought together in God's eternal counsel (Ephesians 1:9-10). This theme continues to build throughout John.

Participating in a wedding celebration, He does a miracle that reveals His glory (John 2:11). The wine ran dry during this celebration, so Jesus created more wine out of water. The master of the feast said to the bridegroom, "Every man at the beginning sets out the good wine, and when the guests have well drunk, then the inferior. You have kept the good wine until now!" (John 2:10). The story points us to Jesus as the Bridegroom of all peoples among who He builds His church (Ephesians 5:30-32). When Jesus returns there will be a wedding celebration called the marriage supper of the Lamb (Revelation 19:6-7). Matthew records Jesus speaking of a feast that many from the east and west will attend with Abraham, Isaac, and Jacob (Matthew 8:11). From that time on, Jesus will reign from Jerusalem over all the earth.

After revealing His glory in the miracle of wine, Jesus headed to His Father's house in Jerusalem (John 2:7-22). As the "Just One" (Acts 7:52), He confronts injustice going on in the temple, referring to the temple as His Father's house. This house is a house of prayer for all peoples (Mark 11:17). Jesus declared His physical body to be the temple. That temple will be filled with some from every people group when He returns (Ephesians 2:19-22). His disciples recalled a phrase from one of David's psalms, "Zeal for Your house has eaten Me up" (John 2:17). By this, He is declaring that He is the entry point for all peoples into communion with their Maker. This same zeal works through His people unto proclaiming the good news, betrothing all who receive Him, and it will result in Him returning and releasing worldwide justice (Isaiah 9:7; 42:13; 59:17).

With zeal for all peoples to be in communion with His Father, Jesus spoke of the Father's love for the world. He communicated this through conversation with a Jewish religious leader named Nicodemus. In response to his question about Jesus' identity, He said "Most assuredly, I say to you, unless one is born again, he cannot see the kingdom of God" (John 3:3). The only way people are born again is through the Spirit by faith in Jesus. Through this, Jesus explained His identity as the One who reveals the love the Father has for all peoples. He had every people group in mind as He proclaimed, "For God so loved the *world* that He gave His only begotten Son, that whoever believes in Him should not perish but have everlasting life" (John 3:16, emphasis added). In love, God sent His Son for the whole world, not just pieces of it. He came as light into a dark place, loving His neighbor as Himself, unto death (John 3:19).

Jesus builds on this truth of the Father's love for all peoples by engaging in conversation with a Samaritan woman. The Samaritans were a group of

Jewish and Gentile descent that "pure" Jewish people did not associate with. A Jewish man conversing with a Samaritan, especially a Samaritan woman, was not the cultural norm of the day. Attempting to move past the awkwardness prompted by the situation with the Samaritan woman, and due to the long journey they had made, Jesus' disciples urge Him to eat some food. Comfortable, Jesus said, "My food is to do the will of Him who sent Me, and to finish His work" (John 4:34). He went on to define the Father's will and work: "Do you not say, 'There are still four months and then comes the harvest'? Behold, I say to you, lift up your eyes and look at the fields, for they are already white [ready] for harvest!" (John 4:35).

Jesus uses the imagery of a field ready for harvest in a Samaritan context to describe the Father's desire for all peoples. His sustenance was to fellowship in the Father's love and invite all people groups into this eternal fellowship. Unashamedly, Jesus declared His intent for the harvest of every people group into eternal fellowship with their Maker. In Matthew, Jesus spoke of the multitudes as a harvest (Matthew 9:35-38), who were Jewish in that context, though He had all people groups in mind. In John 4, Jesus includes the Samaritans as part of the harvest, though they are not fully Jewish. Again, in Matthew, Jesus calls the world a field, made of Jews, Gentiles, and any combination among them (Matthew 13:38). Through the multiplicity of Jesus' statements comes the comprehensiveness of His scope and desire to have all people groups as His inheritance in His Father's eternal family. Speaking of this same desire in varied contexts, Jesus was confronting strongholds in His disciples' minds, and biases we hold toward others who are not like us in language, economic level, geographic location, education level, etc.

In the next several chapters of John, Jesus reiterates a truth that is for all the earth. His scope is the world and His offer is everlasting life for anyone who comes to Him. In John 5, He declares that all judgment is entrusted to Him and everlasting life only comes through Him (John 5:21-24). In John 6, He declares Himself to be the bread of life who came down to give His life for the world, and who will give that life to all who come to Him (John 6:37, 40, 45, 54). He declares, "I am the living bread which came down from heaven. If anyone eats of this bread, he will live forever; and the bread that I shall give is My flesh, which I shall give for the life of the world" (John 6:51).

Later, He says that all who come to Him will receive living waters welling up in them (John 7:37-39).

By using the images of bread and water, Jesus declares Himself to be eternal sustenance for all who come to Him. In John 8 and 9, Jesus describes Himself as the light of the world, saying that all who come to Him have the light of life (John 8:12; 9:39). In John 10, Jesus uses a figure of speech to depict Himself as the Good Shepherd and the gate for the sheep, being the way into the sheep pen (John 10:6-7, 9, 14). He may be referencing Psalm 100, which says, "Make a joyful shout to the LORD, all you lands! Serve the LORD with gladness; Come before His presence with singing. Know that the LORD, He is God; It is He who has made us, and not we ourselves; We are His people and the sheep of His pasture" (Psalm 100:1-3).

Through Psalm 100, we see that all who call upon the name of the LORD are welcomed into His sheep pen. Jesus is the LORD of that sheep pasture, composed of every people group. He said, "Other sheep I have which are not of this fold [Gentiles]; them also I must bring, and they will hear My voice; and there will be one flock and one shepherd" (John 10:16). Jesus came for Israel's lost sheep (Matthew 15:24). He also came for all nations' lost sheep. This truth is clearly expressed again in John 11. He declared Himself to be the resurrection and the life, and said that all who come to Him will live, even though people die physically (John 11:25). He then raised Lazarus from the dead as an example of His power over physical death. Because of this, many Jews believed in Him. Jealous and filled with fear, Jewish leaders were afraid that everyone would believe and follow Him. Then "Caiaphas, being high priest that year, said to them, 'You know nothing at all, nor do you consider that it is expedient for us that one man should die for the people, and not that the whole nation should perish.' Now this he did not say on his own authority; but being high priest that year he prophesied that Jesus would die for the nation, and not for that nation only, but also that He would gather together in one the children of God who were scattered abroad" (John 11:49-52). The word used for nation is *ethnos*, the same word from when Jesus said that the gospel of the kingdom would be preached in all nations (Matthew 24:14). Jesus' death was not only significant and necessary for the Jewish people but for all peoples.

At the onset of John 12, His death for all was one week away. Jesus continued the same focused pattern of giving Himself for the ends of the earth. He rode into Jerusalem on a donkey, partially fulfilling Zechariah 9. Andrew and Philip tell Jesus that some Greeks (Gentiles) wanted to see Him. He responds, "The hour has come that the Son of Man should be glorified. Most assuredly, I say to you, unless a grain of wheat falls into the ground and dies, it remains alone; but if it dies, it produces much grain" (John 12:23-24). Jesus was speaking of His coming crucifixion and resurrection that will produce a harvest from all peoples. His obedient sacrifice disarmed Satan's ability to keep the nations in bondage to sin and fear of punishment and death (John 16:11; Colossians 2:15; Hebrews 2:14-15). Jesus said, "Now is the judgment of this world; now the ruler of this world will be cast out. I, if I am lifted up from the earth, will draw all peoples to Myself" (John 12:31-32).

Preparing to go to the cross, Jesus spent personal time with His disciples, preparing them for the journey's next steps. They had left everything to follow Him. Things were about to change dramatically as they would go from being with Him to being in Him, with Him continuing His mission by the Holy Spirit. The time was drawing near for the gospel to begin its victorious trek to the ends of the earth. In John 13-17, Jesus readies His disciples for this transition.

Jesus strategically passes on what He longs for, in loving relationship with and through His disciples to the entire world. As a loving leader wanting to pass on what is dearest to His heart and what is necessary for His descendants' success before he goes, so Jesus does. In John 13-17, He tells them of the love of the Father for them, His love for them, how they will be empowered to experience this love in relationship with the Spirit, and how from this relationship, they will invite the ends of the earth into the same relationship. In essence, He is telling them His motive behind the great mission to have all nations, and how they will fulfill that mission.

Jesus begins without words and at the lowest place. He washes His disciples' feet as an example of His life laid down for them because He loves them (John 13:1-16). He does this knowing that He has all authority from the Father. He reveals the Father's heart—as One who came to serve, not to be served. The disciples were to love others as Jesus had loved them, keeping this example in mind. This did not mean that they were supposed to wash everyone's feet. It meant they were to consider one another above themselves, as Jesus did for them. The result of this is far reaching—to the ends of the earth. After washing their feet, Jesus said, "A new commandment I give to you, that you love one another; as I have loved you, that you also love one another. By this all will know that you are My disciples, if you have love for one another" (John 13:34-35). God's love is so effective that some people from every tribe will receive Him through His love that they see in His disciples.

The disciples would soon experience this love from the inside out. They had experienced it from Jesus who walked among them, but they would now experience it internally and manifest it externally. Jesus speaks in detail about this internal experience of limitless communion with the Father, Son, and Holy Spirit. He speaks into the human heart's deepest fear and assures us that all who trust in Him do not have to live in that fear. The fear is of being alone, but the assurance is that we are accepted and enjoyed by the Lord, specifically as our Father. The disciples thought they would be alone in the world if Jesus left. He assures them that they will never be alone, but will be infused with the Lord Most High (John 14:1, 16-18, 27). As a man, Jesus experienced the Father's love, and He was inviting His disciples (then and now) to experience the same love.

Developing the disciples' understanding of the intimacy they would experience with Him, Jesus continues by giving an analogy of a vine with branches. The secret to success on the mission is abiding in Jesus the way a branch abides in a vine. A branch does not prosper without the vine. Jesus is not interested in us accomplishing His mission for Him. We do His mission with Him, not for Him (John 15:5). As we abide in Him, He teaches and reminds us of the Father's business (John 15:15). The Father's business is to draw people from every language, tribe, and tongue to His Son. The Father is the Gardener, gathering all nations into the one Vine of His Son. As Jesus' disciples, we abide in His love, agree with His heart's desires, and bear much fruit (John 15:5-8, 16). We did not choose Him but He chooses us and appoints us to go and bear fruit that will last. He appoints us to work with Him as He builds His church, composed of all peoples.

There is much resistance against spreading this intimacy to the ends of the earth. Jesus speaks of this in the second half of John 15 and throughout John

16. However, the kingdom of darkness cannot prevail against the kingdom of light. By fellowship with God and agreement with His desires, the kingdom of light marches victoriously on through the battlefield of this present world (John 16:13-14, 23-27). The main thing Jesus asks of the Father is for the nations to be His inheritance, unto them experiencing the Father's love (John 17:26; Psalm 2:8). As we abide in Jesus, this becomes our desire and prayer.

After speaking these truths, Jesus asks the Father for their fulfillment. John 17 contains Jesus' longest recorded prayer. He is about to freely give His life, that He will be resurrected and seated at the Father's right hand. He desires this so He can give eternal life to all who call on His name (John 17:1-5). He knows He must return to the Father so the Spirit can be poured out on His church to walk with Him and do His will. He prays for His disciples to be strengthened as they are sent to the ends of the earth (John 17:6-19). He finishes by praying for all who will believe the gospel in future generations (John 17:20-25). He has every people group in mind. He prays for the unity of His body as He proclaims His unwavering commitment to declare the Father's name to His church, so we experience His love, remain in Him, and tell the world (John 17:26).

The final statement Jesus made in His prayer sums up His mission and motive behind it (John 17:26). I like to call this Jesus' mission statement. This is the "why" of His mission, and Matthew 28:18-19 and Mark 16:15-18 are the "how" of His mission. He prays, "I have declared to them Your name, and will declare it, that the love with which You loved Me may be in them, and I in them" (John 17:26). Jesus declared the name of the Lord while on earth, and He declares it to this present day through His Spirit, by His ambassadors. This will continue until the gospel has been declared to every people. Revelation of the Lord's name, specifically as Father, through Jesus, leads to experiencing His wholehearted love for us—the same love He has for Jesus. Jesus' motive for declaring the Father as the Lord is to bring the nations into fellowship with Himself, the One from whom, for whom, and by whom creation exists. This is God's eternal purpose for us (Ephesians 1:3-10; 3:11).

Following His prayer, Jesus provides the way, through the cross, for all nations to return to fellowship with their Maker. The Jews gave Him into the governor Pilate's hand. Jesus was crucified and raised from the dead. Following His resurrection, He appeared to His disciples and said to them,

"Peace to you! As the Father has sent Me, I also send you" (John 20:21b). As the Father sent Jesus to Israel's lost sheep, Jesus sends His disciples to the ends of the earth. They walk in the same relationship with the Spirit that He experienced, crossing cultural and language barriers with Christ's love and the power of His kingdom. We are given more detail in the book of Acts on how this sending takes place and how the spread to the ends of the earth began.

In Acts, the author Luke gives an account of how the mission continued after Jesus started it. Jesus went from being on earth as a man to being at the Father's right hand. He transfers His ministry from walking with His disciples to being in His disciples, through the Spirit. From this transfer, Luke details the exponential effect of the spread of the gospel through many, by the ministry of the Spirit in them. This book begins with, "The former account I made, O Theophilus, of all that Jesus began both to do and teach, until the day in which He was taken up…" (Acts 1:1-2). "The former account" refers to his written account of Jesus' ministry, known as the gospel according to Luke. All that Jesus began to do and teach will continue through His church by the Spirit in them until the gospel reaches every tribe. The church is not only to teach the gospel, but to expect God to confirm it with signs and wonders (Hebrews 2:3-4; Mark 16:15-18).

Jesus focused on spreading the gospel to the ends of the earth while the disciples' focus was closer to home. They wanted to know when the Gentiles would no longer have dominion over Jerusalem and the kingdom would be restored to Israel. Jesus told them, "It is not for you to know times or seasons which the Father has put in His own authority. But you shall receive power when the Holy Spirit has come upon you; and you shall be witnesses to Me in Jerusalem, and in all Judea and Samaria, and to the end of the earth" (Acts 1:7b-8). Jesus basically says, "I will clothe you with Myself and you will see things like I do. You will go to the ends of the earth, compelled by My love, to go to who you now see as 'unclean Gentile heathen.' Then My global church will be built and the kingdom will be restored to Israel." He gave the template in Acts 1:8 for His mission's completion. The kingdom will be restored to Israel with that completion.

Jesus modeled the template He gave in Acts 1:8 for the gospel to go to both Jews and Gentiles. He ministered in Jerusalem, Judea, Samaria, and ventured a little beyond Israel. Anything outside of Israel constitutes the ends of the earth. He was sent to Israel's lost sheep (Matthew 15:24). As a physical man, this was His geographic ministry focus. Occasionally, He ministered to Samaritans and Gentiles (John 4:7-26; Matthew 15:21-28). Following His resurrection, He instructed His disciples to preach the gospel and make disciples of all nations: the lost sheep scattered over the whole earth (Matthew 28:18-19; Mark 16:15; Luke 24:47). The template seen in Acts 1:8 takes shape over the decades following Jesus' ascent: "But you shall receive power when the Holy Spirit has come upon you; and you shall be witnesses to Me in Jerusalem [Acts 1:1-6:7], and in all Judea and Samaria [Acts 6:8-9:31], and to the end of the earth [Acts 9:32-28:31]." Notice that the majority of Acts focuses on the ends of the earth.

Jesus kept His promise to baptize His disciples in His Spirit, so the gospel would advance (Acts 1:4; 2:1-4). On Pentecost, the Spirit was poured out on apostles and others. Jews residing in various Gentile lands came to Jerusalem for Pentecost, an annual feast in the Law of Moses. Jews who came from those lands heard the apostles and others, in languages from where they lived, declaring God's wonderful works. This was a sign to them that God knows all languages and that the promise of salvation is for Jews and all who are far off, meaning all Gentiles (Acts 2:17, 39). Those who believed, 3,000 that day, could begin to spread the gospel to the ends of the earth.

At this unusual occurrence, Peter received revelation from the Lord about what was happening. He quoted Joel 2:28-32 (Acts 2:17-21). Joel's prophecy declares that all who call upon the name of the LORD will be saved. This outpouring of the Holy Spirit started on that Pentecost and continues to this present day, preceding the great and awesome day of the LORD (Acts 2:20). The great and awesome day of the LORD refers to the time leading up to Jesus' return, also known as the end of the age. This present age will end when the gospel is preached to all peoples (Matthew 24:14). They cannot call on His name until they hear the gospel (Joel 2:21; Romans 10:17). When the Lord says He will pour out His Spirit on all flesh, He has all peoples in mind (Acts 2:17; John 16:8). There are still people groups who have not received their Pentecost.

In Jerusalem, the gospel continued to spread, but soon met resistance. As the apostles and others followed Jesus' model of preaching, teaching, and healing, the effect was positive for many; but, not believing in Jesus, Jewish leaders persecuted His followers. One of these followers, Stephen, was martyred and many were scattered. "At that time a great persecution arose against the church which was at Jerusalem; and they were all scattered throughout the regions of Judea and Samaria, except the apostles…Therefore those who were scattered went everywhere preaching the word" (Acts 8:1b, 4). Philip is highlighted as a specific example of the gospel going to Samaria and to Gentile areas, further fulfilling Acts 1:8 (Acts 8:5-40).

From there, the gospel pierced Gentile lands. In Acts 10, some Gentiles received the Spirit when Peter preached the gospel to them. Before Peter preached to Gentiles, he received instruction from the Lord that confronted his biases toward people outside of his culture. He learned that God accepts people from every tribe who call on His name (Acts 10:15, 28). He said, "In truth I perceive that God shows no partiality. But in every nation whoever fears Him and works righteousness is accepted by Him" (Acts 10:34b-35). This advance into Gentile lands continued to spread, with a most unlikely individual behind much of the momentum.

Saul of Tarsus, whom most of us know as Paul, went from one of Jesus' greatest enemies, to spreading His fame among many nations. He was a devout Jew who hated Christians and sought to persecute and kill them. After realizing he was persecuting the Messiah promised throughout the Old Testament, he put his trust in Jesus. He spent the remainder of his life growing in understanding of the gospel and spreading it to the ends of the earth. He became fully convinced that Jesus desires all nations as His inheritance. His commission and ambition was preaching Christ in regions that had not heard (Romans 15:20). He knew that Gentiles from every people would receive the gospel when they heard it (Acts 28:28). He received this understanding by revelation from the Spirit, not from his own ideas. He understood God's intentions and Old Testament prophecies: that all nations will be His inheritance.

He connected his ministry to Gentiles to God's promise in the Old Testament that all nations will praise Him for His mercy. For example, on his first missionary journey, Paul spoke in a synagogue in Antioch in Pisidia. Many of the Jews there rejected his message, to whom he said, "It was necessary that the word of God should be spoken to you first; but since you reject it, and judge yourselves unworthy of everlasting life, behold, we turn to the Gentiles. For so the Lord has commanded us: '*I have set you as a light to the Gentiles, that you should be for salvation to the end of the earth*'" (Acts 13:46b-47, emphasis added). On this account, John Piper comments, "In Acts 13:47, Paul's explanation of his ministry to the Gentile nations is rooted in the promise of Isaiah 49:6 that God would make his servant a light to the nations."[14] Jesus calls His church to go to every people on earth (Matthew 28:18-20; Mark 16:15; Luke 24:47). We are to disciple already reached people groups, and to ask God to send laborers from the reached to earth's remaining unreached peoples, until all have heard.

Later, Paul penned a letter to the church in Rome, that expresses God's desire. The letter articulates God's longing for the nations to know Him, and He shows this longing by declaring the gospel through those who know Him. Christ presents Himself to the earth's peoples through those who were lost, and then became reconciled to God (2 Corinthians 5:17-21). The letter of Romans gives us many treasures concerning benefits of salvation in Jesus. These treasures are for every tribe. People receive these treasures as they hear them declared by laborers.

Paul starts the letter with a title identifying his motivation for inviting the nations into fellowship with Jesus. He calls himself a bondservant of Jesus Christ (Romans 1:1). A bondservant serves his master for life–compelled by love. Paul received understanding that Jesus came to serve, giving His life for the entire world (Philippians 3:8-12).

Jesus gave Paul the mission that would affect the ends of the earth forever. He wrote, "Paul, a bondservant of Jesus Christ, called to be an apostle, separated to the gospel of God which He promised before through His prophets in the Holy Scriptures, concerning His Son Jesus Christ our Lord, who was born of the seed of David according to the flesh, and declared to be the Son of God with power according to the Spirit of holiness, by the resurrection from the dead" (Romans 1:1-4). The gospel tells of God becoming fully man while remaining fully God to redeem humanity, bringing them back into eternal fellowship with Him. The Lord called Paul to declare this gospel to all nations. "Through [Jesus] we have received grace and apostleship for obedience to the faith among all nations for His name"

---

[14] John Piper, *Let the Nations Be Glad!: The Supremacy of God in Missions* (Kindle Locations 4002-4008), Baker Publishing Group, Kindle Edition.

(Romans 1:5). "Nations" in Romans 1:5 uses the same Greek word as when Jesus says that the gospel of the kingdom will be preached in all nations as a testimony, and then the end will come (Matthew 24:14). This Greek word, *ethnos*, means tribes or people groups, not current political boundaries.

This gospel Paul preached contains eternal power for all peoples. Paul wrote, "I am not ashamed of the gospel of Christ, for it is the power of God to salvation for everyone who believes, for the Jew first and also for the Greek. For in it the righteousness of God is revealed from faith to faith; as it is written, 'The just shall live by faith'" (Romans 1:16-17). Following this introduction, he explains the effects of all nations falling short of God's glory (Romans 1:18-32; 3:23, 29). Yet God, in His zeal, provided the solution in Jesus' blood (Romans 3:24-26). The theme of Jews and Gentiles both being invited to salvation continues throughout the letter.

This letter of Romans concludes with two main thrusts. One is unity in Christ's body, composed of every people group. Paul prays for a spirit of unity among the church in Rome and tells them to accept one another as Christ accepted them (Romans 15:5, 7). Jesus became a servant of the Jewish people, confirming promises made to them of blessing all nations through them. Gentiles across the earth will glorify God for His mercy (Romans 15:8-12). We are to embrace each other regardless of our earthly heritage, just as Christ embraced us.

The other main emphasis is Paul's desire to take the gospel to unreached places. Paul explains the area he had covered, and his next directional aim. He wrote that he had declared the gospel from Jerusalem to Illyricum, and that geographic region had no more areas for him to work in—so he would visit Rome and head further west to Spain (Romans 15:19, 23-24). Jerusalem to Illyricum, where he had covered, is a vast area from South Palestine to North Italy. Certainly there were many people yet unsaved in this region, and not every individual there heard the gospel directly from Paul's mouth. Additionally, gospel work in the region was young (10-15 years). What was Paul talking about? He focused on Jesus' commission to reach all people groups, not every individual in evangelized areas. These are places where the gospel was proclaimed and a body of believers (church) was created. We do preach the gospel to those in already evangelized areas, but we are also to be ever expanding to villages and cities that have never heard.

The commission the Lord gave Paul to spread the gospel into unreached areas continues today. This commission continues because not all peoples have been reached and they must and will be (Matthew 24:14). The motive for the gospel to go to every people group exists because Jesus gave His life for them and desires to manifest His heart for them through mouths of people who have received Him—with the Holy Spirit testifying. Christ's followers should carry as a primary focus God's overall mission to have all peoples as His inheritance, as this is Jesus' primary focus.

Paul started and finished the letter to the Romans with the same global focus. He began by articulating his commission to call all peoples to obedience to Jesus (Romans 1:5). He ended by giving God glory through Jesus concerning the obedience of all peoples to Him: "Now to Him who is able to establish you according to my gospel and the preaching of Jesus Christ, according to the revelation of the mystery kept secret since the world began but now made manifest, and by the prophetic Scriptures made known to all nations, according to the commandment of the everlasting God, for obedience to the faith—to God, alone wise, be glory through Jesus Christ forever. Amen" (Romans 16:25-27). The letter to the Romans is not mainly about what we have in salvation, but taking what we have to the ends of the earth and inviting every tribe into their eternal inheritance in Christ. Since the world began, God has desired to have each nation as His inheritance. Jesus Christ's death, resurrection, and ascension have made this possible. This becomes reality through preaching the prophetic Scriptures to all peoples.

Jesus provided the way to salvation and the template for how this salvation will reach every people. In Matthew and John, Jesus describes the ever-expanding kingdom, and Acts shows the beginning of this expansion. Paul's desire, in fellowship with God's desire, was to see the gospel reach every tribe. Jesus came and declared that the kingdom was at hand. He secured authority on the cross, taking dominion from Satan. He gave a commission for His disciples to go to all peoples and declare His kingdom. The New Testament shows the ultimate result of the commission as John saw it: "Behold, a great multitude which no one could number, of all nations, tribes, peoples, and tongues, standing before the throne and before the Lamb, clothed with white robes, with palm branches in their hands, and crying out with a loud voice, saying, 'Salvation belongs to our God who sits on the throne, and to the

Lamb!'" (Revelation 7:9b-10). The kingdom expanding into new areas has been and is His foremost aim. Should it not be ours as we abide in Him who redeemed us?

Ben Melancon

Chapter 8

Laborers

In a small trailer, around 15 missions students and I gathered for worship and teaching. As we listened to a missionary from Oman, who ministers to unreached peoples, a vision came to me. It reminded me of Matthew 9, when Jesus looked up from his work, and saw multitudes. He saw beyond their outward appearance. He saw them as harassed and helpless, as sheep without a shepherd. In the vision I saw multitudes of people from different tribes throughout the earth. Their overall countenance was deep sadness, in clothes worn and dirty. There was a sense of darkness and hopelessness over them. They were without hope and without God. The look in their eyes was piercing, and though they did not speak audibly, I could hear the deepest part of them crying out, "Come and help us." I thought of the vision Paul had of a man in Macedonia pleading, "Come over to Macedonia and help us" (Acts 16:9b). I was moved to pray for laborers, in accordance with Jesus' instructions after He saw the multitudes (Matthew 9:36-38). I saw myself in their shoes, and how I would long for someone to come and show me the way to eternal life.

In Acts 16, the Lord gave Paul a vision to redirect him to the fields he was to harvest. The Lord hindered him from entering two other territories before he reached Macedonia: "Now when they had gone through Phrygia and the region of Galatia, they were forbidden by the Holy Spirit to preach the word in Asia. After they had come to Mysia, they tried to go into Bithynia, but the Spirit did not permit them. So passing by Mysia, they came down to Troas. And a vision appeared to Paul in the night. A man of Macedonia stood and pleaded with him, saying, 'Come over to Macedonia and help us.' Now after he had seen the vision, immediately we sought to go to Macedonia, concluding that the Lord had called us to preach the gospel to them" (Acts 16:6-10). Like a farmer who knows where his fields are, when they should be harvested, and how they should be harvested, so the Lord of the harvest knows where each people group is located, the timing to reach them, how to reach them, and through which laborers to reach them. An account from Burma (now Myanmar) demonstrates this.

The year was 1828. Adoniram Judson was an American missionary to Burma. He had come in contact with the Karen people, who lived in remote and almost inaccessible jungles. Judson longed to win a Karen for Christ, and thus open access to these people. This opportunity came through Ko Tha Byu, a Karen slave sold in the bazaar in Moulmein. Ko Tha Byu was a desperate robber bandit. He had been part of approximately 30 murders, and was reportedly a hardened criminal with a vicious nature and uncontrollable temper. Judson worked with this man patiently, prayerfully, and lovingly. Eventually, Ko Tha Byu not only yielded to Christ's transformative power, but went through the jungle as a flaming evangelist to his people. Karens' hearts had been providentially prepared to receive the gospel, via a tradition prevalent among them to this effect:

Long ago, the Karen elder brother and his young white brother lived close together. God gave them each a Golden Book containing what is needed for salvation and joy. The Karen brother neglected and lost his Golden Book and so fell into a miserable way of life. The brother who prized the Golden Book, God blessed. This younger brother sailed away across the ocean, but would return with God's book. If the Karen people would receive and obey that book, it would bring them salvation and blessing. So, as Ko Tha Byu went on his tireless preaching tours through the jungle, declaring that the long-looked-for younger brother [Adoniram Judson] had returned with God's book, hundreds embraced the message with gladness.[15]

Looking at this story and the Acts 16 account, we know that God is overseeing His harvest field, and He harvests it through partnership with His people. The partnership happens by prayer and prayer releases laborers to the harvest fields. Matthew's account says, "When [Jesus] saw the multitudes, He was moved with compassion for them, because they were weary and scattered, like sheep having no shepherd. Then He said to His disciples, 'The harvest truly is plentiful, but the laborers are few. Therefore pray the Lord of the harvest to send out laborers into His harvest'" (Matthew 9:36-38). Imagine you are there with Jesus. He is preaching the kingdom and demonstrating its

---

[15] Daniel L. Akin, *Five Who Changed the World*, 2008.

power. Yet, when He looks up, He sees multitudes and is filled with compassion, longing to help them. I imagine Him saying, "More laborers are needed, until every tribe has the opportunity to accept Me as their Good Shepherd." Through prayer, and multiplication of laborers because of prayer, will come the rich banquet for the wedding of the Lamb, with an array of faces from all peoples present (Revelation 19:6-7).

Matthew 9 unveils Jesus' focus on unreached people groups. The multitudes He saw in Matthew 9 were unreached peoples. Jesus started a world revolution by teaching, preaching to, and healing the lost sheep of Israel. This is the context from which Jesus commands us to pray for laborers. Israel was the starting place of spreading the gospel (Acts 1:8). When we pray for laborers, we want laborers in areas where established groups of believers exist. Yet, we also pray for laborers to be sent to areas where the gospel has not been heard and where there are no established groups of believers. He desires us to go into the entire world, not only the parts that are comfortable or easier to reach.

When Jesus saw the multitudes, He saw beyond broken people living in enmity with each other. He saw beyond Jew and Gentile. He saw their true condition—lack of fellowship with their Maker. He saw the heaviness on their souls and the emptiness of their spirits, dead in transgressions. He saw them as weary and scattered, like a fearful flock of sheep without a shepherd. He longed for them to come to Him as their Good Shepherd and find true satisfaction and rest for their souls. He wanted to heal them of outward infirmities and renew them inwardly. While seeing their brokenness, He also saw them as a valuable harvest.

Jesus saw the multitudes as a plentiful harvest. A harvest is one of the highest delights of life we can experience (Psalm 4:7). In our society, many are detached from depending on harvesting fields, and the reality of seasonal survival. Many go to stores and purchase food year round. This is vastly different than the reality of food supplies getting low as the new harvest approaches. A harvest is valuable in the eyes of those who harvest. Jesus sees the nations as the harvest, more precious to Him than anything in creation (1 John 3:16). Jesus reveals His heart for all peoples when He speaks of Himself as the single seed producing worldwide harvest (John 12:24, 32). He is the seed from which the harvest of eternal life springs up. He began the harvest of eternal life among all peoples by giving His own life.

Filled with compassion, Jesus invites His church to petition the Lord of the harvest to send laborers into the field. As the Master Gardener, the Father is the Master Harvester (John 15:1; Matthew 9:38). He knows where all the fields are, and He has a plan to harvest them. He will not fail and does not get discouraged. As we focus on the Overseer of the harvest, abiding in Him, He fulfills His plans in ways beyond our asking and imagining. If a team of people planned to harvest a huge field of wheat that does not belong to them, they would ask the master about his plan for harvesting. They should follow the plan because the master has authority over his field. The Lord desires a harvest from every tribe, people, and language, and He alone knows the strategy and timing for that harvest. We are called to join Him as His friends, asking Him to send out harvesters.

Jesus tells His church to go and make disciples of all nations while also telling them to ask for laborers (Matthew 28:19; 9:38). So which do we do? Do we major on one and minor in the other? We abide in Jesus and He directs us. Jesus did nothing apart from hearing the Father (John 5:19). He heard the Father by abiding in His love, instructing us to do the same by abiding in Him (John 15:5-9, 15). We focus on Him and He leads us and shows us our part. We then can do our part *with* Him, not *for* Him.

Our primary assignment from God is to abide in Jesus' love, not to pray for and be laborers. As we prioritize this primary assignment, He desires to fill and fuel us to follow His instructions and agree with His desires (John 15:7). Jesus said that we bear much fruit in this way, showing ourselves to be His disciples (John 15:8, 16). The Lord fills us with His desire to pray for laborers because it is His desire (John 15:7). Focusing on our primary identity of abiding in love, we all pray and many are sent to the unreached.

Defining ourselves rightly and pursuing God's primary dream for our lives of abiding in Him enables us to wait patiently on the Lord and trust that our lives will bear much fruit. We are strengthened as we wait upon the Lord, trusting Him to direct our paths (Psalm 27:13-14). We become secure in the Lord's love and do not define ourselves by "our mission or calling" and "great exploits." Scripture abounds with waiting. As we abide and wait, humility grows within as we pray for laborers. Realizing the vastness of the task, we see the power of praying for laborers and the brilliance of God's plan to reveal Himself through many across every language and culture. Harvesting the nations is the work of the body, not an individual. The focus becomes less about "me" and my zeal to do something great and more about the body of Christ and working together with Jesus. If I am a laborer and the Lord gives one more laborer from my agreeing with Him in prayer, then overall fruit multiplies. Laborers increase by agreeing with God in prayer. There are few laborers and much harvest, and I cannot accomplish alone what the Lord wants to harvest. We are to honor Jesus' desire for many laborers. The most practical way we show humility and agreement with Him in this matter is praying for more laborers to be sent.

When Jesus spoke to the disciples about praying for laborers, He was considering the multitudes that He called "the harvest" (Matthew 9:35-38). Jesus longs for multitudes among each people group, not a soul here or there. He longs for mass harvesting. In John 14-17, Jesus spoke to His disciples about the major upgrade and relationship they were about to receive. From this upgrade they would grow in love and through the Spirit in them, many more would become disciples. Within this construct, He repeatedly spoke of the intimacy that comes from asking, believing, and receiving. Out of this comes greater works than Jesus did. He said, "Most assuredly, I say to you, he who believes in Me, the works that I do he will do also; and greater works than these he will do, because I go to My Father. And whatever you ask in My name, that I will do, that the Father may be glorified in the Son. If you ask anything in My name, I will do it" (John 14:12-14). Through this intimacy of asking, the Father is glorified in the Son. The major way the Father is glorified in the Son is through nations coming into His family through the Son, returning to the original design of humanity for fellowship with their Maker.

In context, the greater works Jesus spoke about have at least two dimensions, both with the purpose of Jesus having all nations as His inheritance. One dimension is the increase of greater works by the increase of laborers spreading across the earth. It would no longer be Jesus performing miracles alone, but Him doing so through His church (Mark 16:15-18). This pattern is shown in the book of Acts (2:43; 4:30; 5:12; 6:8; 8:6; 14:3; 15:12; 19:11). The other dimension is that more works than Jesus did will be done through individuals in His church who believe in Him. A main point of God's work in Jesus' day and in His church since has been the harvest of souls. Healings, miracles, etc. point us to the power of God's kingdom, as invitations to receive the good King of the kingdom. Jesus instructed those in His day to believe the works: "If I do not do the works of My Father, do not believe Me; but if I do, though you do not believe Me, believe the works, that you may know and believe that the Father is in Me, and I in Him" (John 10:37-38).

Jesus connected signs with spreading the gospel to unreached peoples: "Go into all the world and preach the gospel to every creature. He who believes and is baptized will be saved; but he who does not believe will be condemned. And these signs will follow those who believe: In My name they will cast out demons; they will speak with new tongues; they will take up serpents; and if they drink anything deadly, it will by no means hurt them; they will lay hands on the sick, and they will recover" (Mark 16:15b-18). During His ministry, Jesus showed the pattern that He desires His people to walk in with Him. Shortly after He spoke of the harvest, He sent His disciples out to the multitudes to heal them and call them to repentance, preparing them to receive the King of kings (Matthew 9:35-38; 10). He continues to send today (Mark 16:15-18).

Jesus gave His disciples power to go to the unreached tribes of Israel, declare His kingdom, and set people free from sickness, demonstrating and confirming the kingdom's power. In Luke, He gave the same power to 70 others to go into the plentiful harvest (Luke 10:1-2). This is the template of how to spread the gospel while interceding for a release of this kind of ministry to the still unreached peoples. Where this pattern occurs, the kingdom of darkness is being defeated. Note the conversation between Jesus and the 70 after their mission: "Then the seventy returned with joy, saying, 'Lord, even the demons are subject to us in Your name.' And He said to them, 'I saw Satan fall like lightning from heaven. Behold, I give you the authority to trample on serpents and scorpions, and over all the power of the enemy, and nothing shall by any means hurt you. Nevertheless do not rejoice in this, that the spirits are subject to you, but rather rejoice because your names are written in heaven'" (Luke 10:17-20). When the gospel is confirmed with signs and wonders as it goes into unreached territory, it is a demonstration of Satan's defeat—his present defeat through Jesus' resurrection and his coming defeat through Jesus' return.

Since those days, the gospel of the kingdom has spread over much of the earth, yet much harvest still remains. At the time of writing this, there are around 7.8 billion people on earth. 3.2 billion of these reside in groups of people where good news of the kingdom is scarcely preached.[16] There are large fields yet to be harvested. There are many among these people who are ready to hear and receive the good news.

With any harvest, there is a beginning, a progression forward, and an end. The same is true in war. The gospel spreading is presented as both a harvest and battle (Matthew 9:36-38; Colossians 1:13; 2 Timothy 2:4). The harvest started with Jesus' earthly ministry and the Holy Spirit outpouring. It has progressed and is now coming to the end. There has been much resistance to the harvest, to the point of bloodshed, as in war. There will be more as the harvest progresses, but for the saints, even in death, there is victory, and the saints will possess the earth forever with Jesus (Revelation 12:10-11).

In the midst of much resistance from the kingdom of darkness, the final stage of the harvest will be completed with great power in the church. The resistance will be fierce because the enemy knows his kingdom will soon be consumed forever, replaced by the kingdom of light that will never be destroyed (Daniel 7:13-14, 26-27; Revelation 11:15). This final push into the remaining harvest field is due to increased intercession for the gospel to go to every tribe.

Throughout church history, renewed focus on mission dawns from renewed focus on prayer. Jesus gave this template in His ministry, and it followed in the book of Acts (Acts 1:4-8; 2:1-4; 13:2). Prayer refocuses us on Jesus' heart. This leads to laborers going into the harvest, teaching, preaching, and healing. Where you see gospel preaching with signs and wonders confirming, eventually conflict ensues as darkness fights against light. I believe we are in the final stage before Jesus' return. This means there will be revival in the church beyond past revivals, resulting in the harvest of the remaining unreached peoples. The number of laborers declaring the gospel and Holy Spirit activity confirming the message with signs and wonders, drawing people to Jesus, is and will be unprecedented since the days of Acts. I invite us to ask the Harvest Chief to release His desire in us to finish the

---

[16] "Global Statistics," https://joshuaproject.net/people_groups/statistics.

mission in our day. May the following story about commitment to what is false and fading provoke the church to focus on what is true and steadfast.

Fire is a sacred symbol dating back to prehistoric times. In ancient Greece it symbolized the creation of the world, renewal and light. It was also the sacred symbol of Hephaestus, and a gift to the human race from Prometheus, who stole it from Zeus. At the centre of every city-state in ancient Greece there was an altar with an ever-burning fire and in every home the sacred Flame burned, dedicated to Hestia, goddess of the family.

Torch Relay races started in ancient Greece as religious rituals held at night. Soon they turned into a team athletic event, initially among adolescents, and further developed to become one of the most popular ancient sports. The enchanting power of fire was a source of inspiration. Sacred flames lit by the rays of the sun always burned in Olympia, in an altar dedicated to Hestia. Fire was ignited with the help of a concave mirror, which has the ability to concentrate the rays of the sun on a single spot. When the head priestess touched that point with the Torch, the Flame was lit.

The Ancient Greeks held a "lampadedromia" (the Greek word for Torch Relay), where athletes competed by passing on the Flame in a relay race to the finish line. In ancient Athens the ritual was performed during the Panathenaia feast, held every four years in honour of the goddess Athena. The strength and purity of the sacred Flame was preserved through its transportation by the quickest means; in this case a relay of Torchbearers. The Torch Relay carried the Flame from the altar of Prometheus to the altar of goddess Athena on the Acropolis. Forty youths from the ten Athenian tribes had to run a distance of 2.5 kilometers (around 1.5 miles) in total.

For the modern Olympic Games the sacred Flame is lit in Olympia by the head priestess, in the same way as in antiquity, and the ritual includes the athletes' oath. The Flame is then transmitted to the Torch of the first runner, and the journey of the Torch Relay begins–its magic still touching people today.

Torch Relay is a non-competitive replication of the ancient Flame relay and a symbolic celebration of the Olympic Games. In a prophetic speech at the end of the Stockholm Games, on June 27, 1912, Baron Pierre de Coubertin said: "And now...people have received the Torch...and have thereby undertaken to preserve and...quicken its precious Flame. Lest our youth temporarily...let the Olympic Torch fall from their hands...other young people on the other side of the world are prepared to pick it up again."[17]

The fire that enchanted the Greek Empire and other cultures is nothing compared to the true light that came to give eternal life (John 1:4). Prometheus stole fire from Zeus, fire that "ever burned" to false gods across the Greek Empire. The Lord is the consuming fire. He baptizes His church with His Spirit. The church is the burning light of the world through Christ. He came to send the fire of His love across the earth. God's family, as torchbearers of His mercy, spread this love through His Spirit. A fire burned across the Greek Empire to the goddess of family. Should not the sacred flame of God Himself burn in the hearts of humankind, from every people (His family) across the earth? David prophesied that it will:

> [27]*All the ends of the world Shall remember and turn to the LORD, and all the families of the nations shall worship before You.* [28]*For the kingdom is the LORD's, and He rules over the nations.* (Psalm 22:27-28)

Laborers of this generation will take up the torch from those who went before them and finish the task. Every four years in ancient Athens, torchbearers carried the torch with fire from the altar of Prometheus to the altar of Athena. Athena is the goddess of wisdom and military victory. The Olympics continue today all over the world, derived from the ancient games. The torch rally is still done in Greece every four years as the Olympics continue at a different location in the world. The torchbearers of the kingdom of God will take His light to every unreached people. The torchbearers will go forth, stewarding all the Lord has given them for the mission, until its

---

[17] "Olympic Torch Relay history and its modern revival," http://intl.2008.cctv.com/20080520/101912.shtml.

completion. God's wisdom will prevail and He will be victorious in His righteousness, humility, and truth.

I believe Coubertin's speech is a call to the body of Christ in this generation: "And now…people have received the Torch…and have thereby undertaken to preserve and…quicken its precious Flame. Lest our youth temporarily…let the Olympic Torch fall from their hands…other young people on the other side of the world are prepared to pick it up again." Since the days of the apostles, each successive generation has received the torch of God's light and the mission has always been, in God's eyes, to take His light to every people on earth. As the church, let us pray and support the spread of the gospel, picking up the mantle of past generations and finishing the task in our day and time. As people focus on the heights of human achievement, may we, as citizens of the kingdom of God, focus on the heights of God's desire and what He is achieving through our agreement.

Consider how Elisabeth Elliot spoke of commitment concerning the mission of reaching unreached peoples: "In a civilization where, in order to be sure of their manhood (or, alas, even their 'personhood'), men must box, lift weights, play football, jog, rappel, or hang-glide, it was startling to realize that there was such a thing as spiritual commitment as robust, as total, and perhaps more demanding than the most fanatical commitment to physical fitness. It was a shock to learn that anybody cared that much about anything, especially if it was invisible."[18] She said this of her husband and several others who went together to unreached peoples in Ecuador.

We are entering final stages of the battle between the kingdom of light and the kingdom of darkness. The resistance is and will be fierce as the gospel, through intercession, goes to every people group. Even so, the One who owns all and has all power will have volunteers. They will preach the gospel to every people and some from every tribe will receive and agree with the Spirit for Jesus to come and be King over the earth (Revelation 22:17). The gates of Hades will not overcome as the God of peace crushes Satan under His feet among every tribe (Romans 16:20). He will then physically return to cleanse the earth of evil and His people will reign with Him forever. As Daniel prophesied,

---

[18] Elisabeth Elliot, *Through Gates of Splendor* (Kindle Locations 2656-2663), Tyndale House Publishers, Kindle Edition.

Then the kingdom and dominion, and the greatness of the kingdoms under the whole heaven, shall be given to the people, the saints of the Most High. His kingdom is an everlasting kingdom, and all dominions shall serve and obey Him. (Daniel 7:27)

Ben Melancon

Chapter 9

The Dominion Mandate

Humility leads to intimacy (friendship) and intimacy leads to dominion. The fellowship of God as Father, Son, and Holy Spirit is built on humility and intimacy, and from that comes His dominion over all. Creation originated from this fellowship, and God's image-bearers were made to live in this fellowship of humility and intimacy, producing dominion that perpetuates life. In the Garden of Eden, Adam and Eve had intimacy and dominion. Choosing pride over staying in fellowship with their Maker, they lost intimacy and dominion.

What humanity lost in the Garden of Eden is in the process of being restored. The effects of rebellion against God are more dramatic than we comprehend, as are the coming effects of humanity's voluntary reception of Jesus from among all peoples. Heaven and earth experienced a separation due to humanity's rebellion. A veil settled over the earth along with an indelible groan that is removed only by the Creator's return (Isaiah 25:7; Romans 8:20-23). According to God's eternal purpose, all things in heaven and earth will be brought together in Jesus (Ephesians 1:9-10). His eternal purpose is for His kingdom and His will to be on earth as in heaven, through reconciling heaven and earth (Colossians 1:19-20). People from every tribe will enjoy fellowship with God. All things will be restored (Acts 3:19-21). This happens through voluntary agreement by people from every tribe with God's desires and plans.

At the beginning of creation, before there was a need for restoration, God made the earth and purposed for it to be filled with those created in His likeness, ruling in fellowship with Him (Genesis 2:15). After forming Adam and Eve in His image, God gave the following blessing and command: "Be fruitful and multiply; fill the earth and subdue it; have dominion over the fish of the sea, over the birds of the air, and over every living thing that moves on the earth" (Genesis 1:28b). On the foundation of fellowship with God, Adam and Eve were to reproduce and fill the earth with the knowledge of His glory. This dominion was always meant to be rooted in fellowship with God.

Adam and Eve chose to disobey God and fell short of the glory of fellowship with Him (Romans 3:23). Exchanging fellowship with the One who has abundant life and is the author of life, they joined in fellowship with Satan, the father of lies who enjoys killing, stealing, and destroying people and all of creation. They chose pride, losing intimacy and dominion. Dominion of the earth transferred from people to Satan (Luke 4:8).

Satan has set his sights on this dominion since the days of Adam and Eve, but his desire will not prevail. God originally gave dominion to people (Genesis 1:26, 28; Psalm 115:16). How then will dominion be restored? How can it be returned to people? On their merits, people cannot return to fellowship with God. They can only be righteous through fellowship with the Righteous One. God made the return to fellowship possible by becoming a man, standing against Satan's lies, and giving His life to take dominion back, providing the way for people to agree with His dominion or to choose to stay in agreement with Satan's failing dominion (Daniel 7:25-26).

Satan's goal in tempting Jesus was to stop Him from taking back dominion of the earth. After failing to persuade Jesus to exalt Himself apart from His Father's leadership, He invited Jesus to worship him in exchange for all the kingdoms of the world (Luke 4:1-8). Jesus was not about to worship the father of lies in exchange for the Father of glory. He was not about to choose pride and lose intimacy and dominion. Rather than choosing self-exaltation by way of pride, He chose lowliness (Philippians 2:6-8). Through humility, He destroyed sin and death that came through Adam and Eve. Losing intimacy with God, Adam and Eve lost dominion of the earth. Jesus restored intimacy and dominion spiritually through the cross (Colossians 2:15). When people from every tribe have heard and some have humbly responded, He will return and restore dominion physically on earth, and His people will reign with Him (Revelation 5:9-10).

By way of the cross, spiritual dominion is granted to all who receive Jesus, and physical dominion follows when Jesus returns. This is why we can grow in holiness all our days through fellowship with God's Spirit and yet our physical bodies still die. Through Jesus, restored intimacy and spiritual dominion in every tribe will give way to restored dominion physically, as in the Garden. As an example, imagine a people group in India, without the hope offered in the gospel. Laborers go to them, declare the gospel, and some embrace Jesus. These new believers receive spiritual dominion over that section of the earth that they inhabit by way of the original blessing (Genesis 1:26). As this happens in every people group, a global invitation for Jesus to return arises (Revelation 22:17). He returns then not by force, but in voluntary response to His beloved among all peoples.

David understood the truth of intimacy with God by way of humility, and the dominion that comes from this. He learned that God's kingdom operates on earth as it is in heaven through voluntary praise from His people (Psalm 22:3). So, by the Spirit's leadership, he instituted night and day worship around the Ark of the Covenant in Jerusalem (1 Chronicles 9:22-23; 28:12-13). David's tent of worship has ceased (Amos 9:11), yet will be restored in fullness when Jesus returns and sits on the throne of David, and Jerusalem becomes the praise of the earth (Isaiah 16:5; 62:6-7; Jeremiah 3:17; Ezekiel 43:7). David's tent is restored by people from every nation, as a global house of prayer (body of Christ) worshipping and praying night and day, leading to Jesus' return (Isaiah 24:14; 42:8-17; Luke 18:1-8). The "spiritual" house of prayer from every people group ushers in physical restoration of God's house of prayer in Jerusalem (Psalm 8; 67; Ezekiel 43:7).

The church, composed of every people group, will welcome back Jesus as King, through worship. Walking in spiritual dominion that Jesus won on the cross, the church will increasingly call out for Him to come as we continue to spread the gospel to the uttermost (Ephesians 3:10-12; Matthew 24:14). Exercising spiritual dominion, by faith in prayer and proclamation, there will come a day when the gospel reaches the final people group and Jesus returns, taking physical dominion over the earth.

We see voluntary agreement from God's people in the book of Ephesians. Paul wrote Ephesians while in a Roman prison. He wrote as one who understood God's master plan and made it the goal of his life to live in agreement with that plan. He was commissioned by God to spread the gospel to the ends of the earth, and lived with the vision of Jesus having all nations as His inheritance. In the first three chapters of Ephesians, Paul focused on God's desire for His church and the authority we have in Jesus as His body.

Before creation, God had in mind heaven and earth being one and all peoples living in eternal fellowship with Him in a restored Eden (Ephesians 1:3-14). Humanity's rebellion did not render His plan useless. It prepared the way for God to reveal the entirety of His wisdom and prudence, through the riches of His grace, given to us not begrudgingly, but freely (Ephesians 1:5-8). He experienced pleasure in wholeheartedly giving Himself for humanity (Ephesians 1:9).

After this introduction, Paul prayed for those who received Jesus to know God and their identity in Him. He desired them to know God more, and to know His eternal calling to fellowship with Him in dominion, to experience Christ in them, and to experience His power over sin and death (Ephesians 1:17-19). Jesus, as the head of the church, rose from the dead and is seated at the right hand of the Father above every principality and power forever (Ephesians 1:20-21). With that backdrop, Paul writes, "He put all things under His feet, and gave Him to be head over all things to the church, which is His body, the fullness of Him who fills all in all" (Ephesians 1:22-23). All things have been put under Jesus' feet, and His church is called the fullness of Christ. Do we understand who Jesus is and do we understand who we are in Him? He is unstoppable.

Though all things are under Jesus' feet, we do not yet see this in fullness (Hebrews 2:8-9). Spiritually, we see the gospel prevailing in its conquest to the ends of the earth. Yet physically, we do not see everything under Jesus' feet. The writer of Hebrews says that Jesus is waiting for His enemies to be made His footstool (Hebrews 10:12-13). He waits in heaven for the gospel to be preached to every people (Matthew 24:14). He makes intercession for the nations to be His inheritance. By way of humility and intimacy with Jesus, we are conformed to His image, making known the effective work of the cross to principalities and powers as the gospel spreads over the earth (Ephesians 3:10-11). Satan is not able to keep any people group from the gospel that Christ came to share. When this is complete, He will physically put His enemies under His feet, on earth as in heaven.

Because of what Jesus did on the cross, we have boldness to enter the Most Holy Place and agree with Him for every people group's salvation (Ephesians 3:12). For this reason, Paul prays for the church to be strengthened through the Spirit, to abide in Jesus' love corporately (Ephesians 3:14-19). He has in mind people groups who are not yet part of Jesus' body. He then exalts God as the One who can do exceedingly above all that we can ask or imagine, according to His power working in us. His glory eternally operates in the church through Christ (Ephesians 3:20-21). Part of the "exceedingly abundant" work that God will do is taking heathen people from every people group, who hate Him, and molding them into His body (Ephesians 2:22). He does this through voluntary agreement from His church.

The book of Revelation ties together and describes the full impact of the church's agreement with God's plan, restoring dominion on earth as in heaven. You may have heard it said that if you want to know what a book is about, read the first few and last few pages. This is true of the Bible when we read Genesis and Revelation. The parts between Genesis and Revelation reveal humanity's utter failing apart from God, and God's faithful commitment to restore humanity and all of creation. The beginning of Genesis expresses the intimacy of God as He creates the heavens and earth, and then people in His own image, to rule over His creation with Him. With freedom of choice, people chose separation from their Maker rather than union. Revelation expresses the intimacy of God and every people group's agreement with this intimacy, leading to the removal of injustice and the return to His original intent.

The book of Revelation is mainly about the beauty of Jesus' leadership and the church's agreement with it, not primarily about strange events, Satan, and persecution of Israel and the saints. It reveals the spiritual dominion of saints in mission and prayer, bringing about the return of Jesus and physical dominion.

The entire book is a prophecy. It is the only book in the Bible that has a specific blessing attached to it for reading it and taking it to heart. Jesus says, "Behold, I am coming quickly! Blessed is he who keeps the words of the prophecy of this book" (Revelation 22:7). "Keep" here means "to attend to and to guard carefully." Jesus invites us to attend to and keep the revelation of Himself before us. Those who add to or take away from it are cursed (Revelation 22:18-19). The book tells of the beauty of Jesus, His coming dominion, the saints' victory with Him, the restoration of the heavens and earth, the demise of Satan, and of all who lived in agreement with him. It tells what will happen before it happens. This gives us stability as we know that there is an appointed end to this present evil.

Satan works diligently to create confusion around the final biblical prophecy, that tells of his demise and the glorious triumph of Jesus and His church. The church is given the prophecy so we can partner with God in prayer to bring about the prophecy's events leading to Christ returning, defeating the kingdom of darkness, releasing worldwide justice, and reigning forever. We are given the plan ahead of time to humbly agree with it, exercising spiritual dominion in prayer and mission, leading to worldwide justice.

In Revelation, we find that the mission Jesus gave reaches its fullness with the saints' prayers. God acts in the earth in conjunction with the few who receive Him and partner with Him because He has entrusted dominion of the earth to people. He acts in response to their agreement or disagreement with Him. For example, He was going to destroy all of humanity with a flood because of their agreement with wickedness. However, because of Noah's agreement with righteousness, He destroyed the earth, but continued His promise of restoration through Noah. In the New Testament, the book of Acts shows that the gospel spreads through saints' agreement with God in prayer. Revelation depicts Satan and humanity's rage against Jesus, His church, and Israel, while also depicting the church in global unity, calling out for Jesus' return and the release of His justice. God's activity in heaven and events on earth correlate with the saints' prayers (Revelation 6:9-12; 8:3-5). With Jesus' leadership, the church's agreement in prayer and mission leads to Him taking the scroll from the Father's hand (Revelation 5:1-9). The scroll points to authority to judge the world in righteousness.

Let's look at the book of Revelation with the paradigm of Jesus' beauty, and the completion of the mission He gave, leading to dominion on earth as in heaven. John magnified Jesus as the One who loved us and gave Himself for us, positioning us with Him to serve His God and Father in everlasting dominion (Revelation 1:5-6). He then described his experience of seeing the glorified Christ and wrote Jesus' words in seven letters to specific churches (Revelation 1-3). Afterward, John is taken up to heaven and sees God's throne, where the eternal, holy Creator sits (Revelation 4). He sees worship in His dwelling place. Then he sees a scroll in the hand of the One on the throne and hears the declaration, "Who is worthy to open the scroll?" (Revelation 5:2b). Other ways to say this are, "Who is worthy to rule over the earth in righteousness? Who is able to know the hearts of all? Who has the ability to righteously judge all and then lead the world in righteousness forever?" John is moved to tears because it appears that no one can fix the injustice of earth (Revelation 5:3-4). Then one of the elders tells John that there is a solution. Someone has prevailed over injustice. He is then directed to behold the Lion of the tribe of Judah, the Root of David. These titles depict Jesus as the King of the Gentiles and the Jews, as King of kings over all the earth.

"The Lion of the tribe of Judah" comes from a prophecy Jacob gave about his son, Judah:

> [8]*Judah, you are he whom your brothers shall praise; your hand shall be on the neck of your enemies; your father's children shall bow down before you.* [9]*Judah is a lion's whelp; from the prey, my son, you have gone up. He bows down, he lies down as a lion; And as a lion, who shall rouse him?* [10]*The scepter shall not depart from Judah, nor a lawgiver from between his feet, until Shiloh comes; and to Him shall be the obedience of the people (nations).* [11]*Binding his donkey to the vine, and his donkey's colt to the choice vine, He washed his garments in wine, and his clothes in the blood of grapes.* [12]*His eyes are darker than wine, and his teeth whiter than milk.*
> (Genesis 49:8-12)

Judah's brothers praising him is a reference to Israel praising Jesus. The Gentile people groups will also praise Him. He will defeat His enemies like a lion defeats its prey. Jacob's words contain an early prophecy of Jesus confronting the nations' rage against His loving leadership (Isaiah 63:1-3; Revelation 19:13).

Concerning the root of David, David is promised an heir who will sit on His throne forever in Jerusalem (2 Samuel 7:12-16). The title probably has its origin in Isaiah 11:10, which mentions the root of Jesse. Jesse was King David's father. Jesse's lineage went back to Abraham, who was given the promise of land, a seed, and all nations being blessed through that seed. The seed who comes through the line of David's physical father will sit on David's throne, and His government and peace will increase forever (Isaiah 9:6-7).

David's throne is called the throne of the LORD (1 Chronicles 29:23). The root of Jesse will rule the entire earth (Isaiah 11:10). Jews and Gentiles will seek Him and creation will be restored under His rule. Taking these two titles together, we see Jesus as the Lion of the tribe of Judah who will bring justice to the ends of the earth as He confronts evil, and He will reign forever in righteousness as the greater David.

John turned to behold the Lion of the tribe of Judah, and saw a Lamb as if it had been slain (Revelation 5:6). Jesus prevailed to take the scroll, as the Lion of Judah and root of David, because He prevailed as the Lamb of God over sin and death. There was no need for John to weep, because the Lamb of God triumphed. He came the first time to take the judgment due to humankind upon Himself, fulfilling all righteousness (Matthew 3:15). He is coming a second time to judge the world in righteousness, to judge the secrets of human hearts and their acceptance or rejection of His love (Romans 2:16; Hebrews 9:28). While preaching in Athens, Paul declared, "[God] has appointed a day on which He will judge the world in righteousness by the Man whom He has ordained. He has given assurance of this to all by raising Him from the dead" (Acts 17:31). John beheld this One who conquers sin and death.

When Jesus takes the scroll, worship erupts as inhabitants of heaven give Jesus the same worship they give the One on the throne (the Father). The four living creatures and 24 elders fall down before Jesus with harps, and bowls full of incense, described as the saints' prayers. They sing of Jesus' worthiness to rule the earth because of His death and purchase of humanity from every people, making them kings and priests to reign on earth with Him (Revelation 5:8-10). A new song proceeds from the living creatures and elders:

You are worthy to take the scroll, and to open its seals; for You were slain, and have redeemed us to God by Your blood out of every tribe and tongue and people and nation. (Revelation 5:9)

They sing it as a prophecy of Jesus' redeeming power over every tribe. There is a time coming when this new song will be fulfilled, when every people receives Jesus' redeeming power. The bowls filled with the saints' prayers are connected with people from every tribe receiving Jesus. There is a time of completion of the mission Jesus gave (Matthew 24:14). I believe the bowls become full when inhabitants from the final tribe hear the gospel and receive Jesus. Then Jesus will take the scroll, judgment events will come, and the kingdom of this world will become the kingdom of our Lord (Revelation 11:15).

Once Jesus takes the scroll from the Father's hand, there are seven seals and seven trumpets that precede Jesus' physical return to earth (Revelation 6; 8-9; 11:15-19). Through these we see Satan's limited power and humanity's united rage with him against God. We also see God's omnipotent power released in conjunction with the saints' prayers. The first four seals show the advance and seeming prosperity of the fourth beast kingdom that Daniel saw (more detail on Daniel is given later in this chapter). The fifth seal depicts those who were slain by the beast's empire for their testimony of Jesus. They ask the Lord how long it will be until He avenges their blood and judges earth's inhabitants. The sixth seal shows God's response to the prayers of the saints who were slain during the fifth seal. The heavens and earth are shaken, and earth's inhabitants hide in holes in the ground, trying to evade the wrath of the Lamb. The seventh seal releases seven trumpets. Before these trumpets sequentially sound, there is silence in heaven for about 30 minutes. This is the time it takes for a Jewish priest to offer incense on the altar of incense. An angel is offering incense along with the saints' prayers (Revelation 8:3-5). Smoke from the incense, along with the saints' prayers ascending before the throne, bring judgments on earth through the seven trumpets.

The first four seals reveal the seeming prosperity of the wicked. The fifth, sixth, and seventh seals reveal the effect of prayer from the saints, and the trumpets reveal God's omnipotent power. The saints are not afraid of God's judgments, but are involved in their release. Their desire for the release of the judgments is not out of a desire for revenge, but for justice. Abiding in the leader of the judgments, they desire God's mercy in the midst of judgment, that many would be invited to repent and turn to Jesus. The nations are and will increasingly rage corporately against Jesus and His church (Psalm 2:1-4; Revelation 11:9; 17:12-14). In this context, the church will call out for Jesus to return and be King (Revelation 5:8-10; 22:17). Thus, He will righteously remove this evil onslaught. He will reign over earth, bringing forth abundant life. The seventh trumpet brings about Jesus' return and prepares the way for the seven bowls that carry the final demise of the kingdom of darkness (Revelation 11:15).

Interspersed between the seals, trumpets, bowls and after the bowls, the prophecy describes aspects of the Antichrist (beast) empire, that empire's defeat, what happens to the saints, their ultimate victory with Jesus, the marriage supper of the Lamb, and the bringing together of heaven and earth. To summarize, the Antichrist wages war against what appears to be a helpless Lamb and the saints. He does this in pride, lost intimacy, and an attempt at dominion by overthrowing the holy, eternal Creator. The Lamb and the saints win by humility and intimacy, leading to everlasting dominion (Revelation 17:14; Daniel 7:18, 26-27). At the seventh trumpet, loud voices in heaven will declare that the kingdoms of this world have become the kingdoms of our Lord, and He will reign forever and ever (Revelation 11:15).

Daniel prophesied of this ultimate victory and everlasting dominion. He spoke of spiritual and physical dominion. Daniel and Revelation are intricately connected. Daniel was written after Israel's exile into Babylonian captivity, in fulfillment of God's word to them through Moses. The Lord told Moses of their scattering from the Promised Land if they chose to live in rebellion against Him. After 490 years of patience, the Lord fulfilled His word, and they were scattered out of Israel. Daniel was written during this period.

Daniel was one of the Jews exiled in the three waves of judgment that came to Jerusalem. He was exiled in the first wave around 605BC. He grew up in a foreign culture that stood opposed to the God of Israel. Babylon attempted to remove Daniel's devotion to the Holy One through a name change, a new language, literature of the culture that worshipped false gods, and a diet opposed to God's law. Yet from an early age, Daniel resolved to seek the Lord wholeheartedly (Daniel 1:7-8). God moved through him mightily as he took this stance. In Daniel we see humility leading to intimacy, and intimacy leading to dominion.

The book of Daniel contains 12 chapters. The first six detail stories that reveal God's power through those who seek Him wholeheartedly. These chapters reveal that God is the One who truly rules. They also give clues about how Daniel set his heart and how he lived from that set heart. Daniel's lifestyle is a template for how we are to live in a "global Babylon," standing against activities that oppose God. These accounts can help give us faith and courage to stand firm, whether by life or death. There will be many "Daniels" (men and women) in the final season leading to Jesus' return (Daniel 11:33; 12:3).

The last six chapters contain four visions that are given to Daniel over a period of around 17 years. The visions reveal that the kingdom of darkness will attempt to prevail against the kingdom of light and will lose. Revelation 11:15 sums up Daniel 7-12: "Then the seventh angel sounded: And there were loud voices in heaven, saying, 'The kingdoms of this world have become the kingdoms of our Lord and of His Christ, and He shall reign forever and ever!'" (Revelation 11:15).

The four visions given over six chapters:

1. Daniel 7: Four kingdoms rise and fall. The kingdom of heaven destroys the fourth kingdom, and remains forever.

2. Daniel 8: The second and third kingdoms are described, along with a depiction of the Antichrist in the fourth kingdom and his destruction.

3. Daniel 9: Israel's future, Jesus' first coming, the Antichrist's activity in the temple just prior to the Second Coming, and his destruction are relayed.

4. Daniel 10-12: The future of Israel between the third and fourth kingdoms, descriptions of the Antichrist in the fourth kingdom, his destruction, and everlasting victory for the kingdom of heaven is described. All of Daniel's visions rise from a central focus on Jerusalem and the seed promised to David, who will rule the earth from Jerusalem.

In the first vision (chapter 7), Daniel sees four different animals that represent four kingdoms rising in the earth. The animals used to describe these kingdoms are wild beasts. They are beastly in their oppression of people generally, and Israel specifically. The four kingdoms Daniel saw are Babylon, Persia, Greece, and the final beast kingdom. The fourth beast Daniel saw could not be described using the imagery of an earthly beast. Here is his attempt: "I saw in the night visions, and behold, a fourth beast, dreadful and terrible, exceedingly strong. It had huge iron teeth; it was devouring, breaking in pieces, and trampling the residue with its feet. It was different from all the beasts that were before it, and it had ten horns" (Daniel 7:7). After seeing the four kingdoms, Daniel sees the courtroom of heaven and the Ancient of Days. The fourth beast is destroyed and One like a son of man comes to the Ancient of Days and is given dominion over the earth with an indestructible kingdom. Though victory is shown, Daniel is deeply troubled by the fourth beast and his destructive activity. "One of those who stood by" in the vision assured Daniel that the beasts will not be victorious, and reiterated heaven's eternal victory, and that the saints will possess the kingdom forever. Just as the former four kingdoms are on earth, so God's kingdom will be on earth.

The Lord gives Daniel this vision for the saints to know the certainty of victory over the fourth kingdom that will come near the time of Jesus' return. Three of the most powerful kingdoms that existed have come and gone (Babylon, Persia, Greece). The Lord tells us the kingdoms ahead of time and lets us see their fall in history to assure us that the fourth kingdom will fall, even though it will be greater and more destructive than the former three, trampling the whole earth (Daniel 7:23). The fourth kingdom will make war against the saints of the Most High but will lose, as there is coming judgment from the Ancient of Days, in favor of the saints (Daniel 7:21-22, 27). The saints are from every people group and emerge from the time of the great tribulation (Revelation 7:9, 14).

In chapter 8, Daniel is shown a war between the Persian and Greek kingdoms (second and third beast kingdoms). The Greeks are victorious. From the Greek kingdom will come a "little horn" exalting itself against the Holy One of Israel. This little horn is the leader of the fourth beast empire (Daniel 7:7-8; 8:9-11). The little horn and fourth empire spring up at the time of the end (Daniel 8:17). Revelation gives more detail about this fourth kingdom (Revelation 12-13; 17).

In chapter 9, Daniel is found studying the Scriptures. He reads about the 70 years prophecy from Jeremiah and understands that the time is near for its fulfillment. The Lord promised to restore the Jewish people to Jerusalem after 70 years of exile. Daniel commences a time of prayer and fasting in agreement with God's word. Toward the end of this time of prayer, the angel Gabriel comes to Daniel to give him insight into Israel's future. Connected to the 70 year captivity, Gabriel tells Daniel of 70 weeks that come before Jerusalem's full restoration. Each week refers to seven years. The 70 weeks therefore cover 490 years, the same number of years Israel was in the Promised Land before they were scattered for their ongoing rebellion. The 70 weeks or 490 years are broken into seven weeks, 62 weeks, and one week. The first seven weeks refer to Daniel's present day when the Jewish people went back to Jerusalem and rebuilt it. The 62 weeks refer to when Jerusalem is rebuilt, up to Jesus' first coming, when He was crucified. The last seven refer to when the fourth beast kingdom's leader makes a covenant with many peoples (Daniel 9:27). In the middle of the seven years, he breaks the covenant and sets himself up in the temple in Jerusalem and declares himself to be God (2 Thessalonians 2:1-4). He also sets up what is called "the abomination of desolation," a type of idol.

The visions in Daniel connect the abomination of desolation with the appointed end, as Jesus does (Daniel 9:26-27; Matthew 24:3, 14-15). Jesus also connects the completion of preaching the gospel to this same season (Matthew 24:14). The beast, with the nations, will rage against God, His church, and Israel. The saints will hold to the testimony of Jesus and pray according to God's plan as they declare the gospel to every people. Jesus will take the scroll from the Ancient of Days, the beast kingdom will be judged and destroyed, and the saints of the Most High will possess the kingdom forever with Him (Daniel 7:18; Revelation 11:15).

In Daniel 10-12, Daniel is given understanding of what would happen a couple centuries after the fall of the Greek kingdom (third kingdom), and what will happen at the end with the fourth kingdom (Daniel 10:14). The vision Daniel saw gives detail about military campaigns surrounding Israel, over a couple centuries after the death of Alexander the Great, the leader of the Greek kingdom. These events occurred historically. God knows the future, so we can be assured that the fourth beast kingdom will rise and fall as well. The nations are as nothing before Him (Isaiah 40:17). The end of chapter 11 and beginning of 12 show that the fourth beast's rage and the tribulation occur simultaneously. The beast will come to an end and Israel will be delivered (Daniel 11:45-12:1).

Jesus connects the time of tribulation and abomination spoken of by Daniel to the gospel going to every nation, and His second coming (Matthew 24:3, 14-31). After His resurrection, He spoke of "things pertaining to the kingdom of God" (Acts 1:3b). The disciples asked Him when He was going to restore the kingdom to Israel (Acts 1:6). Jesus told them that it was not necessary for them to know, but that they would be His witnesses, starting in Jerusalem and on to the ends of the earth (Acts 1:8). It is implied that the kingdom will be restored to Israel when the gospel has gone to every people on earth. In the Scriptures and in the Jewish mindset, Israel is the center of the nations and Jerusalem is the place God chose to rule from. In the days of Jesus, though Israel was in the land of Canaan, they did not have control over the land. Rome did. This is why the disciples wondered when the kingdom would be restored to Israel. Daniel's visions comfort and assure us that the kingdom will be restored to Israel, and Jesus will reign forever.

The restoration of the kingdom to Israel happens in the context of some from all people groups welcoming Jesus to be king over the earth from Jerusalem. In the midst of this, many will rage against the Lord and His Anointed One. While Daniel gives some detail of the four kingdoms, Revelation focuses on the rise and fall of the fourth kingdom.

Three specific titles Jesus uses in the book of Revelation convey His authority over all and the certainty of His kingdom prevailing over the fourth beast kingdom (Revelation 1:8, 11, 17; 21:6; 22:13). The three titles are "the First and the Last," "the Beginning and the End," and "the Alpha and the Omega." They are used at the beginning and end of the prophecy. They are used to point back to prophecies in the Old Testament, specifically those of Isaiah and Daniel. These titles and aspects of the prophecies surrounding them tie together the gospel going to every people group, the rise and fall of the four kingdoms, and the ultimate victory of the Lord's kingdom.

In the days of Hezekiah, the Lord said that Babylon will remove Israel from her land (Isaiah 39:5-7). This did not happen for another 150 years or so. The remaining chapters of Isaiah prophesy Babylon's demise at the hand of Persia. Mingled throughout are prophecies of Jesus' first and second comings, the salvation of Gentile peoples, and judgment of people who rage against Jesus. In Isaiah 40-49, we find that the Lord knows the end from the beginning, unlike the false gods of the peoples. He declares that He is the First and the Last. He does not specifically call Himself the Beginning and the End, but speaks much about the beginning and no one but Him knowing the future. Daniel saw the kingdoms of Babylon, Persia, Greece, and the fourth kingdom that rises at the end of the age (Daniel 7). Isaiah 40-49 deals with the first two kingdoms, Babylon and Persia. When Jesus uses the titles "the First and the

Last" and "the Beginning and the End," He is saying that He is the LORD who is the salvation of all peoples and who knows the end from the beginning. He knew that Persia would destroy Babylon. He spoke it before it happened through Isaiah and Daniel (Isaiah 41:4; 44:6; 46:10; 48:3, 5, 12, 16).

The other title Jesus used, not referenced in Isaiah, is "the Alpha and the Omega." It is also not referenced in Daniel, though I suspect that Jesus had Daniel's prophecies in mind when He used the title. The third kingdom Daniel saw was Greece, who defeated Persia. The title "the Alpha and the Omega" comes from the Greek language. Looking at Daniel, the Antichrist seems to rise out of the remnant of the Greek Empire (Daniel 8:17-25). Alpha is the first letter of the Greek alphabet, and Omega is the last letter. During that time, Greece was known for its wise thinkers. It was a place of human wisdom. This was still evident centuries later when Paul went through Athens (Acts 17:16-21). When Jesus says He is the Alpha and the Omega, I believe He is saying something like, "I am the beginning and the end of true wisdom. I know the whole story from the beginning to the end. Just as Babylon and Persia came and fell, so Greece has come and has fallen. Be assured that the final empire Daniel saw will also rise and fall."

These three titles are used to express to the church and the raging nations that He who spoke of the rise and fall of Babylon, Persia, and Greece will Himself defeat the fourth kingdom. The kingdom of God will overtake the kingdom of this world, and Jesus will reign forever and ever (Revelation 11:15). Daniel testifies to this:

> *[13]I was watching in the night visions, and behold, One like the Son of Man, coming with the clouds of heaven! He came to the Ancient of Days, and they brought Him near before Him. [14]Then to Him was given dominion and glory and a kingdom, that all peoples, nations, and languages should serve Him. His dominion is an everlasting dominion, which shall not pass away, and His kingdom the one which shall not be destroyed...*

> *[26]'The [heavenly] court shall be seated, and they shall take away his dominion [Antichrist and fourth kingdom], to consume and destroy it forever. [27]Then the kingdom and dominion, and the greatness of the kingdoms under the whole heaven, shall be given*

to the people, the saints of the Most High. His kingdom is an everlasting kingdom, and all dominions shall serve and obey Him.' (Daniel 7:13-14, 26-27)

People from every tribe knowing Jesus will precede His return, and full restoration of dominion will ensue through prayers of the saints. The Eden humanity is trying to get back to will be fulfilled. Fellowship with God, who is love, will be fully restored.

Chapter 10

Love

A trip into an Indian village led me to an encounter with the love of Christ for all the peoples of the earth. The road was a mixture of pavement and soil, worn down by years of travel. On this road, there were more traveling by foot than by car. After some time walking, an Indian friend and I came into the center of a village. We proceeded down a pathway, stopped, and stepped inside a family's home to visit them. Several people lived there in a one room, smaller than the average American bedroom. According to outward appearance, life seemed poor and hopeless. Food was not plentiful. But with the Lord's perspective, I saw beyond the physical. I saw that these people were no different from me, and I no different from them. My heart burned with the love of Christ for them.

Across large stretches of the earth, cities and villages are inhabited by multitudes like you and me. We are common, ordinary people who are made in the image of God and are precious in His sight. Our source of existence is God's eternal love. We have families, we work, we grow hungry and thirsty, and we experience moments of joy and periods of sorrow and pain. We have thoughts, feelings, and desires. These unreached, unengaged people are like you and me, except they have not found eternal life. They are held in bondage to the power of Satan, and God desires to set them free (Acts 26:18). He desires to set them free just as He set us free. He desires to do this through you and me. We have been given the chance to return to the source of our existence—fellowship with the one true God who is love. Compelled by this love, we invite people to fellowship with Him.

The Lord of the harvest reaches all people groups in a rather ordinary way. He reaches them through you and me, ordinary people created in the image of God and for His glory. Jesus, as the first laborer, became a man to reach the lost sheep of Israel, a people sitting in darkness (Matthew 4:15-16). In His kindness He called them to come to Him. Through His disciples, who were transformed by His love, they began to call the peoples surrounding Israel to repentance. They went to others who were different by language, skin color, culture, gods, etc. But inwardly all are the same, in need of a Savior to fulfill the longing of eternity in our hearts—to know that we are loved completely. Down through the centuries, the church has expanded. In the same transforming love, the church is still growing and calling people to repentance unto experiencing His marvelous lovingkindness (2 Corinthians 5:17-21). This continues until the gospel is declared to all peoples.

God showed humankind how much He loved them by giving His life for them (Romans 5:8; 1 John 3:16). The first and greatest commandment is to love God with our all and the second is like it, to love our neighbors as ourselves (Matthew 22:37-40). God does not require us to follow a command that He does not exemplify. He fulfilled the law by becoming a man and loving us as Himself (the second commandment). Abiding in Him, His love moves through us (Galatians 5:13-14; Romans 13:9-10).

From Jesus' perspective, what is behind His command to love our neighbor as ourselves? How did He, as a man, love His neighbor as Himself when He walked the earth? How did He love all peoples? How did He love all who were around Him and all future generations? He came to the unreached people group of Israel and reached them. He invited them into eternal fellowship with their Maker. He baptized His disciples in the Holy Spirit and told them to do as He had done (Matthew 28:18-20). Looking at Jesus' commission, and His focus when He walked the earth, practical ways we can love our neighbors are praying, sending resources, training, and/or going ourselves to people groups who have not had a witness of Jesus. We can love our neighbors by preaching the good news to them, beckoning them into eternal life (2 Corinthians 5:17-21).

Wherever we are geographically, we are to focus on reaching those peoples that remain with no gospel witness. This does not necessarily mean we personally go to them, but we should be aware of Jesus' focus and point others to that focus. I am not minimizing loving our neighbor on a daily basis with our words and actions, nor am I saying that it is not good to reach people sitting in darkness in already evangelized areas. I am offering a biblical narrative on God's mission and heart for unreached peoples. Since it is His primary pursuit, it should be a primary pursuit of the global body of Christ. He does not return until the mission is completed. Paul longed for the coming of Christ and was compelled by His love to go to the ends of the earth to call people into fellowship with God (2 Corinthians 5:14). As the Spirit reveals the love of Christ to us, we are compelled to go where He leads and share His love with others. Love is our motivation for going to unreached peoples—the love of Christ Himself. This is what Jesus did, even unto death, and He gave us the commission to do the same. Abiding in Him, should we expect anything different?

Jesus Christ becoming a man was the ultimate manifestation of the second commandment to love our neighbors as ourselves (Matthew 22:37-40). It is concrete evidence of our worth in God's eyes (John 15:9). Jesus is fully God and He became a man. As a man, the Spirit of God moved through Him to reconcile the world to Himself. He took the judgment due us upon Himself (Isaiah 53:5). This is love, defined by God (1 John 3:16). Paul wrote, "God was in Christ reconciling the world to Himself, not imputing their trespasses to them" (2 Corinthians 5:19). He does the same through us: "Now then, we are ambassadors for Christ, as though God were pleading through us: we implore you on Christ's behalf, be reconciled to God" (2 Corinthians 5:20).

Called to reconcile people to God, we no longer judge by outward appearances and accomplishments. We no longer assume things about people and put them in brackets based on culture, skin color, education level, economic status, family line, etc. When we do that, we are not abiding in the love of God (1 John 2:9-10; 4:20). The Spirit, working through Paul, said it this way: "For the love of Christ compels us, because we judge thus: that if One died for all, then all died; and He died for all, that those who live should live no longer for themselves, but for Him who died for them and rose again. Therefore, from now on, we regard no one according to the flesh. Even though we have known Christ according to the flesh, yet now we know Him thus no longer" (2 Corinthians 5:14-16). Before knowing Jesus, we regarded Him according to the flesh. We presumed that Christ's life was weak and foolish. He did not pursue greatness the way people pursue greatness. He did not determine success by lineage, education, or economic status. He did not base His life on what people thought about Him and what they wanted for Him or from Him. But when His great mercy and love were revealed to us, we saw

Jesus' life as wise, beautiful, and holy. We no longer regard Him according to outward appearance as we once did (2 Corinthians 5:16).

Being set free from our self-sufficiency and worship of self, we look past the outward and see people as equal, and lost in darkness apart from Jesus. We see them through the lens of love, through the eyes of Christ. He made all peoples and laid down His life in love for them. They were all created in His image and He came to spread the fire of His love to all of them.

As ministers of reconciliation, we are to no longer regard anyone after outward appearances. He who had no sin became sin for us, regardless of our culture, skin color, or anything else that people would put in categories of better or worse, higher or lower, richer or poorer. He did this so we could be saved and become the righteousness of God in Him (2 Corinthians 5:21). Knowing this truth, we can be impartial and go anywhere the Lord leads us, and plead with people to be reconciled to God (2 Corinthians 5:20).

A major aim of the sanctifying work of the Spirit is to work out of us our impartiality toward others. Most, if not all of us who are new creations in Christ, have pockets of prejudice from our old nature. Prejudice means having wrong attitudes, feelings, and opinions regarding certain person(s) or group(s). Prejudice is of a nature desiring to harm with words and actions rather than build up in love. Sadly, this explains at least some of the reality that, specifically in the United States, the most segregated hours of the week are when the body of Christ gathers to worship.

Allowing prejudice to grow leads to racism. Racism is valuing one group over another to the point of oppressing the other group. Racism at its base is not about one race or tribe being superior but about pride and envy. Racism is founded in comparison, wondering who is better than another. It results in harming our neighbors rather than loving them. It is a direct attack against the knowledge of God who made all peoples in His image. This comparison of one another is in direct opposition to God, who is love. Paul warned against this in the church, writing, "For you are all sons of God through faith in Christ Jesus. For as many of you as were baptized into Christ have put on Christ. There is neither Jew nor Greek, there is neither slave nor free, there is neither male nor female; for you are all one in Christ Jesus" (Galatians 3:26-28). Peter wrote, "Honor all people" (1 Peter 2:17a). John wrote, "If someone says, 'I love God,' and hates his brother, he is a liar; for he who does not love his brother whom he has seen, how can he love God whom he has not seen?" (1 John 4:20). When we consider ourselves better than others, we are not walking in the Spirit and are blinded to God's call to go to all people groups. If we are unwilling to be changed from this heightened view of ourselves, we may need to seriously consider if our faith is really in Jesus Christ, or in "another gospel."

Consider God and His behavior toward us. He is love, and all creation proceeded from His wholehearted love. He is unbounded in power and resources. His greatness cannot be fathomed and His understanding is without limit. He is high and holy, while also being gentle and lowly. As the Lord God Almighty, He still invested Himself fully in making us. He became a man, giving His life freely for us. He enjoys considering us above Himself. He loves us as Himself. This was revealed in Jesus becoming a man, not to be served but to serve. We are to have the same mind as Christ. Though God, He made Himself nothing. Then He humbled Himself, becoming obedient unto death on a cross. He became a curse for us. Through this pathway He is exalted (Philippians 2:5-11). This is how God walks out love. Therefore, we are instructed as His ambassadors to do nothing out of selfish ambition or conceit but in lowliness of mind to esteem others as better than ourselves (Philippians 2:4). Consider the apostle Peter. Even after being filled with the Holy Spirit he had a difficult time making the transition, walking in the truth that Jesus desires Gentiles as much as He does Jews and that God is focused on heart transformation, not on outward appearance or things we do to approve ourselves before God (Acts 10:28; Galatians 2:11-16).

As God considers me, loving me while a sinner, so I am not to demean people through all my comparisons, in my mind or with words. I am not to consider a wealthy, educated person as better than a poor, uneducated person (James 2:1-4). I am not to consider a doctor or scientist as better than those who cannot read. I am to joyfully consider all as better than myself.

Seeing who God is, His commitment to me, and His pursuit of me, I do not have to see people as projects to improve, nor be intimidated by people who see me as a project to improve. Nor do I have to lord anything over others to feel comfortable in my authority. I can be confident in God's love for me and this is the governor and motivator of all I say about and do toward others. Seeing others through God's eyes becomes a wonderful adventure and makes life a delight. Each person is seen through compassion and as a unique image-bearer of God. Learning about them as I hear their stories—their defeats and victories, is a joy and a delight. I do not judge them by outward appearance. My desire in Christ is to love them, not compare to them or harm them.

When we see who God is and how He sees us, it is incredibly silly and deceptive to put people on different levels in our minds and act toward or against them according to our own categorizing. We should ask God for His mind, and eyes to see the potential He sees in all peoples. The unreached people group that Jim Elliot longed to reach was considered savage by most. One of the missionaries who died with him, Pete Fleming, wrote, "I am longing now to reach the AUCAS if God gives me the honor of proclaiming the Name among them...I would gladly give my life for that tribe if only to see an assembly of those proud, clever, smart people gathering around a table to honor the Son—gladly, gladly, gladly! What more could be given to a life?"[19] Notice how he saw them with the eyes of Christ: proud (in a positive sense), clever, and smart while others saw them as savages.

Walking in love, Jesus tells us of the strong resistance we will experience while harvesting with Him. He experienced much resistance and said the same would be true for us (John 15:18-16:4). When we experience hatred from people because of the gospel, it reveals hatred for the Maker (John 15:23; 16:3). When Paul persecuted Christians, he persecuted Jesus. Listen to his account: "When we [Paul and those with him] all had fallen to the ground, I heard a voice speaking to me and saying in the Hebrew language, 'Saul, Saul, why are you persecuting Me?...' So I said, 'Who are You, Lord?' And He said, 'I am Jesus, whom you are persecuting'" (Acts 26:14-15).

We are not to be surprised by hatred toward us (1 John 3:13). The Spirit of glory rests on us (1 Peter 4:12-14). The words of the Eternal One are clear: "They will deliver you up to tribulation and kill you, and you will be hated by all nations for My name's sake" (Matthew 24:9). Those who resisted Jesus the most were actually the ones called to lead people to Him. The Jewish leaders of the day did not receive Jesus. They labeled Him "Beelzebub," the leader of demons (Matthew 10:25)! Disciples of Jesus should not be surprised by similar accusations. A disciple is not above His teacher, but all who are

---

[19] Elisabeth Elliot, *Through Gates of Splendor* (Kindle Locations 260-264), Tyndale House Publishers, Kindle Edition.

fully trained will be like their teacher (Luke 6:40). As we abide in the love of Jesus and walk with Him where He goes, we fellowship in His suffering while experiencing His joy (John 15:9-11; Matthew 10:25).

Jesus actively pursues His enemies and teaches us to do the same as we abide in His love. He said, "You have heard that it was said, 'You shall love your neighbor and hate your enemy.' But I say to you, love your enemies, bless those who curse you, do good to those who hate you, and pray for those who spitefully use you and persecute you, that you may be sons of your Father in heaven; for He makes His sun rise on the evil and on the good, and sends rain on the just and on the unjust. For if you love those who love you, what reward have you? Do not even the tax collectors do the same? And if you greet your brethren only, what do you do more than others? Do not even the tax collectors do so? Therefore you shall be perfect, just as your Father in heaven is perfect" (Matthew 5:43-48). We are to love, bless, and pray for those who curse us and use us. This is how we fight and how the kingdom of God advances. We do this through Christ in us, not in our own strength.

Being fully God and fully dependent on the Spirit in Him, Jesus revealed God perfectly and teaches us to walk the same path. We do so through abiding in His complete love (1 John 2:5-6). We are called to be perfect as our heavenly Father is perfect (Matthew 5:48). Perfect means complete or mature. Perfect is not about never making a mistake. It is about abiding in the love of Christ as the primary pursuit of our lives. We abide in His completion (Colossians 2:10; 1 John 4:12-13, 17-18). As we do this, transformation is guaranteed. We will pursue those who hate us. We will gladly go to all peoples, knowing that they are sheep that Jesus desires to rescue, bringing them into the green pastures of eternal life.

The nations, agreeing with Satan, rage against God's love. Satan has been a murderer from the beginning because there is no truth in him. Jesus calls him the father of lies (John 8:44). The reason for Satan's hatred is his own pride and separation from God. As he deceives the nations, this continues to lead to much killing, stealing, and destroying until Jesus returns. Satan's plan is to take over heaven and earth and to keep humanity under his bondage. His plan failed at the cross (Colossians 2:15). His destination is the lake of fire prepared for him and angels who became loyal to him (Matthew 25:41). Unwilling to surrender, and moving in the fullness of everything opposed to

God's light, he rages against God's plan to rule with people over the earth. This is why he fights against the spread of the gospel to every people group. Satan's hatred, along with the pride of humanity in agreement with him, has been a major cause of war amongst fellow humankind since the beginning.

The original plan was for people to walk in fellowship with the Lord in love, free from shame and fear. This fellowship happens through confident dependency on and consistent dialogue with God. The result would have been peace, rest, and security. War would not exist. Through Jesus, the earth will return to this original plan. Without this dependency, the nations continue to act like brute beasts toward one another outwardly, while inwardly they are shivering orphans without the shelter and confidence of the loving Father.

Daniel prophesied that war will continue until the end, and Jesus spoke of peoples rising against peoples and kingdoms against kingdoms (Daniel 9:26; Matthew 24:7). Their rage culminates in openly making war against Jesus at His second coming (Zechariah 12:1-3; 14:1-3). They will be defeated and the leadership of the earth will be given to the saints (Daniel 7:26-27; Revelation 19:19-21). Jesus will bring an end to war. As a Psalmist declared, "He makes wars cease to the end of the earth; He breaks the bow and cuts the spear in two; He burns the chariot in the fire. Be still, and know that I am God; I will be exalted among the nations, I will be exalted in the earth!" (Psalm 46:9-10).

As the church, we are not to be alarmed by war, nor are we to fight the way the world fights—in their wisdom, riches, and strength apart from God. We are to fight as Jesus did when He walked the earth—in the power of His love. We are to fight in His gentleness and meekness. As Paul wrote, "Now I, Paul, myself am pleading with you by the meekness and gentleness of Christ...For though we walk in the flesh, we do not war according to the flesh. For the weapons of our warfare are not carnal but mighty in God for pulling down strongholds, casting down arguments and every high thing that exalts itself against the knowledge of God, bringing every thought into captivity to the obedience of Christ" (2 Corinthians 10:1a, 3-5).

We focus on God's kingdom and righteousness (Matthew 6:33). We are to represent His kingdom through the Holy Spirit's power as we walk in love, even toward our enemies (Matthew 5:43-48). In the midst of wars all across the earth, we are to fear no evil because God is with us (Psalm 23:4). We are to stand against fear and all the evil that comes from acting in fear. We stand against fear by standing in the perfect love of Jesus (John 15:9; 1 John 4:18). We are to go to all the unreached peoples, knowing that some of them will war against us, but there are within them those who will hear and declare, "Worthy is the Lamb who was slain!"

As I have been writing, the hymn "Onward, Christian Soldiers" (below) has come to mind. This is a hymn the Salvation Army adopted. When we see "Salvation Army," let us think of still unreached peoples, and the church as an army fighting with faith, love, and the confidence of victory. God's love never fails and thus, His plan will not fail (Psalm 33:10-11; Proverbs 21:30). Jesus Christ is the judge of the living and the dead, and He invites us to return to Him. The supreme ruler who has power to condemn only condemns those who refuse His everlasting love (Romans 8:33-34). For those who receive Him, nothing in all creation can separate us from His love (Romans 8:35-39).

Onward, Christian soldiers, marching as to war,
with the cross of Jesus going on before.
Christ, the royal Master, leads against the foe;
forward into battle see His banners go!

Refrain:
Onward, Christian soldiers, marching as to war,
with the cross of Jesus going on before.
At the sign of triumph Satan's host doth flee;
on then, Christian soldiers, on to victory!
Hell's foundations quiver at the shout of praise;
brothers, lift your voices, loud your anthems raise.

Like a mighty army moves the church of God;
brothers, we are treading where the saints have trod [and onward
to unreached peoples].
We are not divided, all one body we,
one in hope and doctrine, one in charity.

Crowns and thrones may perish, kingdoms rise and wane,
but the church of Jesus constant will remain.
Gates of hell can never 'gainst that church prevail;
we have Christ's own promise, and that cannot fail.

Onward then, ye people, join our happy throng,
blend with ours your voices in the triumph song.
Glory, laud, and honor unto Christ the King,
this through countless ages men and angels sing.[20]

---

[20] Sabine Baring-Gould, "Onward Christian Soldiers," Public Domain, 1871.

Part 3
Your Part in the Story

Chapter 11

The War Offensive

"One of the things that surprised me when I first read the New Testament seriously was that it talked so much about a Dark Power in the universe—a mighty evil spirit who was held to be the Power behind death and disease, and sin. The difference [between Christianity and Dualism] is that Christianity thinks this Dark Power was created by God, and was good when he was created, and went wrong. Christianity agrees with Dualism that this universe is at war. But it does not think this war is between independent powers. It thinks it is a civil war, a rebellion, and that we are living in a part of the universe occupied by the rebel. Enemy-occupied territory—that is what this world is. Christianity is the story of how the rightful King has landed, you might say landed in disguise, and is calling us all to take part in a great campaign of sabotage."[21]

As Christians on earth, we live in enemy-occupied territory, yet we have power within us that cannot be defeated, even by death. We are in this world, but not of this world (John 17:14-16). In Jesus, we have overcome every spirit who sides with Satan and speaks his lies through the mouths and actions of humanity. John said, "Beloved, do not believe every spirit, but test the spirits, whether they are of God; because many false prophets have gone out into the world. By this you know the Spirit of God: Every spirit that confesses that Jesus Christ has come in the flesh is of God, and every spirit that does not confess that Jesus Christ has come in the flesh is not of God. And this is the spirit of the Antichrist, which you have heard was coming, and is now already in the world. You are of God, little children, and have overcome them, because He who is in you is greater than he who is in the world. They are of the world. Therefore they speak as of the world, and the world hears them" (1 John 4:1-5). Notice here that the enemy fights against the identity of Christ,

---

[21] C.S. Lewis, *Mere Christianity* (1952. Harper Collins: 2001), 45-46.

the rightful inheritor of earth that Satan has possessed since Adam and Eve's rebellion. Notice also that he is unseen, yet releases his lies through people who live in agreement with him.

In a similar way, God is unseen, yet He releases His truth through people who live in partnership with Him. Satan uses people maliciously, trying to achieve his goal of dethroning God. In love God invites humanity to partner with Him, to crush Satan and usher in everlasting righteousness on earth.

Indeed, there is a real battle around us, more intense than any physical battle—it is the clash between the kingdom of darkness and the kingdom of light. The primary goal of the kingdom of darkness is to stop Jesus from returning and taking over leadership of the earth. To do this, the enemy knows that he must stop the spread of the gospel to every people, because this unlocks the door that brings Jesus' return (Matthew 16:18; 24:14). Satan is the parent of evil. Evil manifests itself in the physical realm by people's agreement with it, resulting in war against flesh and blood, driven by principalities and powers. Goodness originates in God and reveals itself in the physical realm through people who abide in Jesus, fighting with weapons of meekness and gentleness against principalities and powers (2 Corinthians 10:1-5; Ephesians 3:10-12; 6:12-17). Sometimes their own blood is shed by the hands of those who agree with darkness, but believers know that it is more than worth it.

If we are to engage in the battle around us, we must really believe that there is a battle. As Christians, we should perceive this present world as a world at war. If we don't, how will we live with a sense of urgency, or labor diligently with Jesus for the fulfillment of His mission? In wartime, all efforts are directed toward the war. What we do with time and resources is vastly different depending on if we live in a time of peace or a time of war. Peacetime is coming! But apart from clear vision of the current, ongoing battle, we get overly focused on the temporary and the petty. We spend time and resources excessively on things that do not support the spread of the gospel to every people group. We take pride in earthly citizenship, get comfortable with our surroundings, and try to make our lives secure for the future and live for weekends, holidays, and vacations. Yes, God gives us created things for our enjoyment (1 Timothy 6:17). However, the amount of time, energy, and resources that go into them can easily lessen our focus on the mission God has given us.

There is a type of sacrifice that we choose to embrace as we choose to be led by Jesus rather than leading our own lives; and in the sacrifice, we discover internal and external provision that the world knows not of. Sacrifice was not a barrier for Jesus, because of His confidence in the Father's love for Him, because of the joy of having all peoples as His inheritance, and because He knew that death had no power over Him. We often think of sacrifice as loss, but maybe we should think of it more as gain (Philippians 3:7-12). As David Livingstone said, "If a commission by an earthly king is considered an honor, how can a commission by a Heavenly King be considered a sacrifice?"[22]

Jesus tells us that His word can be choked out by the cares of this world and the deceitfulness of riches, making it unfruitful (Matthew 13:18-23; Luke 8:14). Inordinate amounts of time spent on maintaining the cares of this world and trusting in riches does not help spread the kingdom. As John Piper said, "I am wired by nature to love the same toys that the world loves. I start to fit in. I start to love what others love. I start to call earth 'home.' Before you know it, I am calling luxuries 'needs' and using my money just the way unbelievers do. I begin to forget the war. I don't think much about people perishing. Missions and unreached people drop out of my mind. I stop dreaming about the triumphs of grace. I sink into a secular mind-set that looks first to what man can do, not what God can do. It is a terrible sickness. And I thank God for those who have forced me again and again toward a wartime mind-set."[23]

Paul also viewed life in this age as a fierce war. This was not youthful zeal from his early days that faded with the passage of time. No, he carried this mindset into his last days. Referencing Paul's final days, John Piper wrote, "When Paul came to the end of his life, he said in 2 Timothy 4:7, 'I have fought the good fight, I have finished the race, I have kept the faith.' In 1 Timothy 6:12, he tells Timothy, 'Fight the good fight of the faith. Take hold of the eternal life to which you were called.' For Paul, all of life was war. Yes, he used other images as well—farming, athletics, family, building, shepherding, and so on. And yes, he was a man who loved peace. But the pervasiveness of war is seen precisely in the fact that one of the weapons of

---

[22] John Piper, "'I Never Made a Sacrifice,'" Desiring God, March 19, 2018. https://www.desiringgod.org/articles/i-never-made-a-sacrifice.

[23] John Piper, *Don't Waste Your Life* (Crossway, 2018).

war is the gospel of peace! (Eph. 6:15). Yes, he was a man of tremendous joy. But this joy was usually a 'rejoicing in the sufferings' of his embattled mission (Rom. 5:3; 12:12; 2 Cor. 6:10; Phil. 2:17; Col. 1:24; cf. 1 Peter 1:6; 4:13)."[24]

Paul told his spiritual son Timothy to stir up the gift of God that was in him through the laying on of Paul's hands and also to wage the good warfare through prophecies about him (2 Timothy 1:6; 1 Timothy 1:18). He was saying something like, "Timothy, you have the Spirit of God in you. You have the love, power, and sound mind of God. God is available within you. You must do your part, Timothy. God will not manifest His power, love, and sound mind in and through you without your partnership. Enter into prayer. Remember and agree with the prophecies made over you. Enter into fellowship continually and you will grow strong in the grace that is in Christ Jesus."

The Spirit of power, love, and a sound mind in us drives fear away as we "stir up" the gift of God within us (2 Timothy 1:7). This stirring is not from doing more outward activity. It is from the humble movement of our heart toward God. This is how we grow strong in grace (2 Timothy 2:1). Paul was reminding Timothy that this is how we walk as good soldiers of Jesus Christ: "You therefore must endure hardship as a good soldier of Jesus Christ. No one engaged in warfare entangles himself with the affairs of this life, that he may please him who enlisted him as a soldier" (2 Timothy 2:3-4). Through growing strong in God's grace, with love that casts out fear, we face the war. There is no need to fear, for we are in the One who has overcome this world and who will return to reign forever.

Being citizens of the kingdom of heaven while living on earth as aliens, we are in enemy territory. Jesus has bestowed His Father's kingdom upon us, entrusting us with the assignment to spread the news of this kingdom to every people group. In the war effort, every person has a job, or a part, and all the parts make up the whole.

The main ways we are involved in the mission are praying, going, sending resources, and making others in the kingdom aware. There are many and varied ways of how this plays out. A mother may pray often for the finishing

---

[24] John Piper, *Let the Nations Be Glad!: The Supremacy of God in Missions* (Kindle Locations 1151-1156). Baker Publishing Group. Kindle Edition.

of the mission, for specific missionaries, and for revelation of the mission to become clearer to the church, while teaching her children about Jesus and His mission. A young person prays earnestly to be sent and finds himself in a training school, and then going into an unreached people group. Another person has a business where she works as to the Lord, while focusing on funneling profits to fund the mission. A pastor may have many initiatives in his local congregation, with a priority on missions to the unreached, having this as a foundational truth that is recognized and entwined in all other initiatives.

A military analogy shows how these all work together and are all essential. In war, enemies take over territory. For example, in World War II, Germany took over surrounding European countries. Those who opposed them were called the Allied Powers. These Allies embarked on a military offensive to drive the enemy out of the areas they had seized. This was an arduous task that included significant manpower and supplies. The infantry pushed back the enemy on the ground step by step, mile by mile. The air power supported the infantry by softening the resistance with bombs. Behind the infantry were teams of medical personnel who took care of the injured as they came off the front lines. Masses of people provided food, weapons, and replenished the infantry. All of this involved growing, manufacturing, training, and transporting. It was not only the military involved, but nearly all sectors of society within the Allied Powers. In the same way, everyone has roles they serve in as a part of the kingdom of light. You cannot win a war with just the people on the front lines. What happens behind the front lines enables the front lines to move forward, taking enemy territory. One part is not more important than the sum total of the parts. We abide in Jesus and our part is done through Him, and it is the part He wants us to enjoy with Him (Matthew 28:20; Ephesians 2:8-10).

We have been given a kingdom and a mission, and there is resistance to this mission. The enemy seeks to sidetrack us from this mission in many subtle ways. We will discern these as we make it our primary aim to fellowship with the Lord of the harvest. He will keep us and deliver us from the evil one and his ways. He will give us the daily bread of His word to strengthen us and keep us on mission. A fellow laborer in the war effort provides a fitful summary: "God is pursuing with omnipotent passion a worldwide purpose of gathering joyful worshipers for Himself from every tribe and tongue and people and nation. He has an inexhaustible enthusiasm for the supremacy of His name among the nations. Therefore, let us bring our affections into line with His, and, for the sake of His name, let us renounce the quest for worldly comforts and join His global purpose."[25]

[25] John Piper, *Let the Nations Be Glad!: The Supremacy of God in Missions* (Kindle Locations 1080-1082), Baker Publishing Group. Kindle Edition.

Chapter 12

Going

"I looked back at Bobby, who was steering the boat, and smiled. How strange that I had gotten to this place, that I felt the way I did about these people. It was God who had brought me. I never would have come myself. And even if I had wanted to, I never would have made it past all these problems, past the loneliness, past the danger. In fact, I never would have left my home in Minneapolis if I had not had His powerful, determined Presence inside me."[26]

This is the testimony of a man who grew up in the United States and felt called to a specific unreached tribe in South America. People are called by the Lord with a specific mandate to go to unreached people groups. This was true of Bruce Olsen. Jesus came to unreached peoples in Israel, and He chose 12 apostles to begin going to the rest of the earth's unreached. Paul and Barnabas were also set apart by the Spirit to go to the unreached.

Those called to go as laborers to live among the unreached are like infantry called to the front lines. They go into enemy territory, where there is no witness of the gospel. Their goal is to proclaim and pray, and go with Jesus as He delivers people from the enemy. In this way, Jesus builds His church and the gates of Hades do not prevail against it (Matthew 16:18). They go, armed with the salvation, righteousness, and truth of Christ in them, walking with the gospel of peace that crushes Satan (Ephesians 6:12-18; Romans 16:20). With breastplates of faith and love and the hope of salvation as a helmet, they do not war against flesh and blood, but against principalities and powers that hold people captive to do the devil's will (1 Thessalonians 5:8). Carrying meekness and gentleness, they tear down strongholds over people's mind (2

---

[26] Bruce Olson, *Bruchko: The Astonishing True Story of a 19-Year-Old American, His Capture by the Motilone Indians and His Adventures in Christianizing the Stone Age Tribe* (Kindle Location 7), Charisma House. Kindle Edition.

Corinthians 10:3-6), and by their love for one another, others come to know and join their ranks (John 13:34-35).

In a war, there are often many campaigns going on simultaneously, requiring the infantry to be in different locations. In World War II, there were various infantry groups spread across Europe and the Pacific Islands. These infantries were given specific assignments from military authorities and governments of which they were citizens. The body of Christ is given specific assignments, ultimately from our Commander in Chief Jesus Christ. These assignments come in varied ways and we humbly walk these out together.

Paul received a specific assignment from the Lord, yet it was broad at the same time. Jesus told Paul that He would send him to Gentiles. Specifically, Paul had a mandate to go to regions where the gospel had not been proclaimed (Romans 15:20-21). This journey took place over decades and through the Holy Spirit's leadership (Acts 13:1-2; 16:6-12). His specific mandate involved a vast geographical span and multiple people groups. This was possible through people working together, with each one doing his or her part. The Philippians supported Paul financially. The saints traveled to and from Paul with supplies, encouragement, and letters. People stayed in places where Paul had preached the gospel, to help grow the disciples and make more disciples.

A modern example comes out of India. I know a man who grew up as an orphan in a Christian home in northern India. He received Jesus and went to Bible school. During his time there, he had a vision with the name of a village written in gold letters. He learned that the name he saw was a village in southern India. In obedience, he traveled there with only a suitcase. He did not know anyone and there was no church there. This was in the 1980s. The village and that region were unreached.

He spent a year there with little prayer, a lot of evangelism, and no converts. Afterward, he began to give himself to prayer and after two years, had two disciples. As the years passed he faced much opposition. Patiently enduring through many trials, he now has a house of prayer, 400 people who have come to know Christ in that village, 15 other churches in surrounding villages, and three orphanages. He went to a specific village in obedience to God and reached unreached peoples.

As many veterans in natural wars can attest, casualties on the front lines are high. But in the kingdom of God, physical death does not mean defeat but ultimate victory. What the world may consider loss, the church sees as gain. Without proper perspective, the loss on front lines looks like a waste. Yet Jesus tells us that we are all called to give up our lives as we follow Him. This starts long before physical death. We do this every day as we follow Him while some yield their bodies freely unto death, as Jesus did. Paul died daily many days before he was martyred (1 Corinthians 15:31). We "waste" our lives each day in the sense that we all give our passion to something. Nate Saint, a missionary to an unreached Ecuadorian tribe in the 1950s wrote: "People who do not know the Lord ask why in the world we waste our lives as missionaries. They forget that they too are expending their lives...and when the bubble has burst, they will have nothing of eternal significance to show for the years they...wasted."[27]

Jesus paid the ultimate price and calls us to follow His example. He calls us to see Him and abide in Him, looking beyond what we can physically see and into the eternal, knowing that He will raise us up at the last day just as He was raised up and lives forever (2 Corinthians 4-5; Revelation 1:17-18). Jesus willingly gave His life because He knew it would result in people from every tribe eternally experiencing the same love for them that the Father has eternally had for Him (John 10:17-18).

Nate Saint also wrote about expendability: "During the last war we were taught to recognize that, in order to obtain our objective, we have to be willing to be expendable...This very afternoon thousands of soldiers are known by their serial numbers as men who are expendable...We know there is only one answer to our country's demand for what we share in the price of freedom. Yet, when the Lord Jesus asks us to pay the price of world evangelization, we often answer without a word. We cannot go. It costs too much.

"God Himself laid down the law when He built the universe. He knew when He made it what the price was going to be. God didn't hold back His only Son, but gave Him up to pay the price for our failure and sin.

"Missionaries constantly face expendability. Jesus said, 'There is no man that hath left house, or brethren, or sisters, or mother, or wife, or children, or

---

[27] "Blog," Grace Church, https://bath.graceohio.org/thought-of-the-day-from-nate-saint.

lands for my sake and the Gospel's but shall receive hundred fold now in this time and in the world to come eternal life.'"[28]

Are you called to go? Sincerely pursue the Lord and you will know if you are called to go to the unreached. This may unfold and become clearer over time. Be patient, pray, and follow each stepping stone that is put before you. Whether you are called to go or not, He will cause your heart to burn for His mission as you desire to follow Him fully.

Words that have brought me much solace and encouragement come from Jim Elliot, when he wrote to his friend Pete Fleming about going to the unreached: "I would certainly be glad if God persuaded you to go with me, but if the Harvest-Chief does not move you, I hope you remain at home. To me, Ecuador is an avenue of obedience to the simple word of Christ. There is room for me there, and I am free to go. Of this I am sure. He will lead you too, and not let you miss your signs. The sound of 'gentle stillness' after the thunder and wind have passed will be the ultimate word from God. Tarry long for it. Remember the words of Amy Carmichael: 'The vows of God are on me. I may not stay to play with shadows or pluck earthly flowers, till I my work have done and rendered up account.'"[29]

You will know your part(s) as you trust in the Lord with all your heart and lean not on your own understanding. Whatever your part is, walk it out with your whole heart.

Going is an essential part of the mission, yet not the only part. The amount of front line laborers sent and the quality and effectiveness of those laborers are dependent on prayers of the saints from all parts of the body.

---

[28] Elisabeth Elliot, *Through Gates of Splendor* (Kindle Locations 625-632), Tyndale House Publishers, Kindle Edition.
[29] Ibid. (Kindle Locations 184-189).

Chapter 13

Praying

"The man or woman at home who prays often has as much to do with the effectiveness of the missionary on the field, and consequently with the results of his or her labors, as the missionary."[30] As we do our part, we bear fruit together. Jesus connected prayers of the saints to the release of laborers into His harvest (Matthew 9:36-38). He invites all to pray for the Lord of the harvest to send out harvesters into the field. All are qualified for this work of prayer.

In keeping with the military analogy, prayers are like fighter planes. They release power from above. Since the invention of planes, they have shaped the course of wars. The possibilities of attacking the enemy have greatly increased. As the infantry marches, they sometimes meet heavy resistance. Fighter jets go ahead of them and soften the resistance. Through fellowship with the Spirit, the saints enter into intercession with praise before God's throne. God releases His activity on earth as it is in heaven, thwarting the enemy's purposes. Ways are then opened for the infantry to move forward with the gospel, and God confirms their proclamation with signs and wonders. One of Paul's prayers sums this up well: "Continue earnestly in prayer, being vigilant in it with thanksgiving; meanwhile praying also for us, that God would open to us a door for the word, to speak the mystery of Christ" (Colossians 4:2-3a).

Jesus gives us powerful promises concerning prayer. We can approach God's throne of grace through Christ. We can confidently approach the throne where the eternal, omnipotent, holy Creator sits (Hebrews 4:16). We can do this because Jesus not only cleansed us from our sin by His blood but lifted us to the dignity of being co-heirs with Him as children of His Father (Romans 8:16-17; Revelation 1:5-6). He teaches us to pray while keeping in focus the throne and the Father who sits there, who is pleased to give us His kingdom

---

[30] R.A. Torrey, *The Power of Prayer and the Prayer of Power* (Raven Books, 2013).

(Matthew 6:9-13; Luke 12:32). We are invited to believe God's promises and abide in the One who intercedes for their fulfillment (Hebrews 7:25; Matthew 21:22).

Being in Jesus, we have a high place of abiding that is above every principality and power of this present world. We pray to the Father from this position. We are complete in Christ who is head over every power (Colossians 2:10). He is victorious over sin and death as He sits at the Father's right hand. We are seated in Him there while simultaneously He is in us here on earth (Ephesians 2:6; Colossians 1:27). As we prioritize abiding in Jesus, we commune and the Spirit prays through us, full of abounding hope, completely confident that God's promises will prevail. God will have laborers and His gospel will extend to the ends of the earth.

Individually, we can reach only so many. Yet from our place of abiding, we can reach all the unreached through prayer as we petition the Lord to send out workers to every tribe. Who believes this? Who will tarry long, confident in the love of God and the desires of His heart?

Jesus connects bearing much fruit to prayer (John 15:7-8). Fruit we bear from prayer includes a transformed life, resulting in other transformed lives. Prayer arises from abiding and is a communion of exchange, like a vine and branch. This communion is not only words, but He does love communication with words. So we ask. Consider Jesus' foremost request of the Father: for the Father to reveal Himself through the Son, that all nations would come into the love He has for them (John 17:20, 26). Another way to say this is that Jesus' foremost request is to have the nations as His inheritance. In the whole of the Old Testament, this is the request that the Father invites Jesus to make (Psalm 2:7-8). The Father is glorified as we live a life of communion with Him and proclaim His kingdom in word and action (John 14:12-14; 15:7-8). These sound to me like loving the Lord with our all and loving our neighbor as ourselves (Matthew 22:37-40).

In John 13-17, Jesus shares what He does in expectancy of having some from every people group as His inheritance. He invites us to connect with the Father through the Spirit in the same way He did as a man. He wants us to know that we can experience friendship and relationship, like He experienced with the Father as He walked the earth. We have the same access to the Father that Jesus did while on earth (Ephesians 2:18). We are invited to ask for anything as we abide in Jesus' love (John 14:12-14; 15:7-8; 16:23-27). We ask big with His global mission on the forefront of all we do. This makes whatever part we play exciting. We ask for wealth as we move in the marketplace unto funding the movement of laborers to the unreached. We ask for millions of souls as laborers go and preach to them. We ask for wisdom on how to train laborers and raise awareness in the church.

We get to abide in the same affections and experience the same emotions that Jesus did from His Father. We are valued, accepted, and enjoyed by the Father in the same measure He values, accepts, and enjoys His Son. Through this experience, we can walk as Jesus walked—in confident relationship. We also get to know the yearning of God for those He made in His image, feeling the compassion of God for the nations to know Him.

Prayer, arising from abiding in Jesus, is the main engine that debilitates the enemy and makes a way for the gospel to spread to all peoples. From the place of fellowship with God rises intercession with praise, silencing the foe (Psalm 8:1-2). Abiding with the One who ever lives to intercede leads to agreement with His intercession, bearing much fruit. Discipling the nations is the product of abiding in the love of Jesus and agreeing with His intercession. This is the picture given by Jesus with the vine, branches, and fruit. Fruit is produced on branches, yet branches are completely dependent on the vine. The saints get the honor of abiding in Jesus and through them He gathers all peoples as His inheritance. John 15:16 tells us that Jesus chose us to go and bear fruit. John Piper comments, "The grammar of John 15:16 implies that the reason Jesus gives them their mission is so that they will be able to use the power of prayer. 'I appointed you that you should go and bear fruit...*so that* whatever you ask the Father in my name, he may give it to you.' This is just another way of saying that prayer is a wartime walkie-talkie. God designed it and gave it to us for use on a mission...Prayer is designed to extend the kingdom into fruitless enemy territory."[31]

With His vision of having all nations as His inheritance, Jesus taught about the power of believing prayer for this to become reality. In one of these instances, the week before His death, He drove out moneychangers in the Jerusalem temple and declared, "My house shall be called a house of prayer"

---

[31] John Piper, *Let the Nations Be Glad!: The Supremacy of God in Missions* (Kindle Locations 1221-1225), Baker Publishing Group, Kindle Edition.

(Mark 11:17b). During that time He also cursed a fig tree that was bearing no fruit, though it was not the season for it to bear fruit. The disciples were amazed that the tree withered and Jesus used this to invite them into the power of believing prayer:

> *¹²ᵇWhen they had come out from Bethany, He was hungry. ¹³And seeing from afar a fig tree having leaves, He went to see if perhaps He would find something on it. When He came to it, He found nothing but leaves, for it was not the season for figs. ¹⁴In response Jesus said to it, "Let no one eat fruit from you ever again." And His disciples heard it. ¹⁵So they came to Jerusalem. Then Jesus went into the temple and began to drive out those who bought and sold in the temple, and overturned the tables of the money changers and the seats of those who sold doves. ¹⁶And He would not allow anyone to carry wares through the temple. ¹⁷Then He taught, saying to them, "Is it not written, 'My house shall be called a house of prayer for all nations'? But you have made it a 'den of thieves.'"*
>
> *¹⁸And the scribes and chief priests heard it and sought how they might destroy Him; for they feared Him, because all the people were astonished at His teaching. ¹⁹When evening had come, He went out of the city.*
>
> *²⁰Now in the morning, as they passed by, they saw the fig tree dried up from the roots. ²¹And Peter, remembering, said to Him, "Rabbi, look! The fig tree which You cursed has withered away."*
>
> *²²So Jesus answered and said to them, "Have faith in God. ²³For assuredly, I say to you, whoever says to this mountain, 'Be removed and be cast into the sea,' and does not doubt in his heart, but believes that those things he says will be done, he will have whatever he says. ²⁴Therefore I say to you, whatever things you ask when you pray, believe that you receive them, and you will have them."* (Mark 11:12b-24)

Jesus seems to use cursing the fig tree as a word picture of what was happening in national Israel. In conjunction with driving out people in the temple and cursing the fig tree, He told Jewish people that they had made His house of prayer a place of personal gain. They rejected Jesus as the leader of the house of prayer for all nations, and He told them that they would not see Him again until they declared, "Blessed is He who comes in the name of the LORD" (Matthew 23:39b). In the same week, Jesus spoke of a fig tree again while talking about events that will surround His second coming: "Learn this parable from the fig tree: When its branch has already become tender and puts forth leaves, you know that summer is near. So you also, when you see all these things, know that it is near—at the doors!" (Matthew 24:32-33). In resurfacing the fig tree, Jesus may actually have been referring back to the fig tree He cursed around the time He disrupted the ungodly activities around the temple. There, the fig tree no longer bore fruit because it died. If the two are connected, the fig tree will come back to life around the time of Jesus' second coming. At the end of the age, the Jewish leaders will accept Jesus as Messiah and He will return to Jerusalem, restore the house of prayer for all nations, and reign forever from Jerusalem (Isaiah 16:5; Jeremiah 3:17; Ezekiel 43:6-7). What does this have to do with believing prayer and the gospel going to every people group?

Israel rejected their Messiah, and the gospel began going to the ends of the earth after His death and resurrection. They rejected Him throughout His ministry. At the beginning of His ministry He confronted the ungodly activity in the temple (house of prayer) (John 2:14-21). Then He declared His death and resurrection, speaking of the temple as His body, composed of Jews and Gentiles. Toward the end of His ministry, He again disrupted ungodly activity in the temple and then spoke of the Jewish leaders' rejection of Him and the spread of the gospel, during that same week (Matthew 21:12-16, 28-45; 22:1-14; 23:39; 24:14).

Currently, Jesus' house is spiritually comprised of those from people groups who have received Him (John 2:16-21; Ephesians 2:22). Before His return, some from all people groups will receive Him. I believe the specific context of the invitation to believing prayer in Mark 11:20-26 is believing with Jesus for all peoples as His inheritance, resulting in His return, Israel's salvation, the restoration of David's tent (night and day worship), and Jerusalem being made the praise of the earth (Isaiah 62:6-7; Amos 9:11; Matthew 24:14). Many Jews are and will be saved before this through faith in

Jesus, and Israel will be saved as a whole when He returns (Romans 11:25-26).

Matthew 21 includes the same account of Jesus cursing the fig tree and talking about the power of believing prayer. A few years ago, I was meditating on the promise Jesus offers in Matthew 21:22: "Whatever things you ask in prayer, believing, you will receive." During that time I felt the Lord say, "Who has entered the depths of this verse?" This does not mean that no one has entered the depths of this promise. It was an invitation from the Lord to believe Him at His word and to ask Him to work in His church the anointing of prayer that prevails; in this case, prevails to finish world evangelization. Do you believe God's own desire? Do you believe in the invitation He gave to His Son for all peoples to be His inheritance? Let us then tarry in confidence with the eternal intercessor at the right hand of the Father. Work this truth in us Lord, so we can intercede with You.

Jesus told us that the harvest of people groups is rooted in prayer (Matthew 9:37-38). This is the template given in Joel's prophecy and confirmed in the book of Acts. Joel prophesies of the Holy Spirit's outpouring in the last days. Those last days started with the charge given by Jesus to go to the ends of the earth. The Holy Spirit gives clarity to this through Peter (Acts 2:17-21). Peter mentions this prophecy after Jesus tells the apostles to tarry in prayer in Jerusalem until the Holy Spirit is poured out on them (Luke 24:49). In Joel's day, Israel turned from the Lord. As a result, a plague of locusts devoured the land, affecting food production; so the grain and drink offerings were cut off from the house of the Lord. The state of agriculture in Israel was a statement of where their hearts were with the Lord. The locusts were a precursor to a worse invasion from surrounding nations, if Israel did not repent. The solution was for Israel to turn to the Lord, rending their hearts before Him and not their garments (Joel 2:12-17). The Lord would pour out His Spirit and restore Israel if they would turn to Him with all their heart (Joel 2:28). Peter interprets the "afterward" of Joel 2:28 as the "last days" in Acts 2:17. The apostles followed the prescribed model the Spirit had given through Joel and that Jesus gave them—to tarry in prayer. As a result the Spirit was poured out on them and then on 3,000 more (Acts 2:1-4, 38-41). The gospel has been spreading since then, in the context of the saints' unified prayers. As Samuel Zwemer said, "The history of missions is the history of answered prayer."[32]

A major part of answered prayer for the spread of the gospel is the movement of personnel and resources. Laborers must have finances for daily needs, Bibles, etc., as they move into unreached territory. They also need care and assurance, which comes in varied forms such as written messages and phone calls. Paul the apostle was often encouraged and financially sowed into by others as he pushed into unreached areas. In the next chapter, we will look at sending resources.

---

[32] Samuel M. Zwemer, *Taking Hold of God: Studies on the Nature, Need and Power of Prayer* (Marshall, Morgan & Scott, 1936).

Chapter 14

Sending Resources

"Go therefore and make disciples of all nations, baptizing them in the name of the Father and of the Son and of the Holy Spirit, teaching them to observe all that I have commanded you. And behold, I am with you always, to the end of the age*" (Matt. 28:19–20). The implications of this are huge for the way we live and the way we think about money and lifestyle. One of the main implications is that we are 'sojourners and exiles' (1 Peter 2:11)…We do not use this world as though it were our primary home. 'Our citizenship is in heaven, and from it we await a Savior, the Lord Jesus Christ' (Phil. 3:20). This leads to a wartime lifestyle. That means we don't amass wealth to show the world how rich our God can make us. We work hard and seek a wartime austerity for the cause of spreading the gospel to the ends of the earth."[33]

Biblically, the point of wealth is for God's glory to be revealed to nations. God releases power to get wealth in order to establish His covenant with Abraham (Deuteronomy 8:18). Part of the covenant includes some from every people being blessed with salvation through Christ and being brought into His eternal kingdom that will rule on earth. God releases His blessing that His ways may be known in the earth (Psalm 67). As citizens of heaven living as pilgrims in this present age, we can believe God for wealth for the finishing of the mission He gave us. Money and resources are ingredients that God uses as His people work with Him. Jesus received money and resources as He spread the message of the kingdom throughout Israel (Luke 8:3). As we are serious about finishing the mission, the Lord will see to it that resources are provided (Proverbs 13:22; 28:8).

In war, those on the front lines do not last if they are not supported and encouraged by those from the homeland. As saints, our homeland is with God and we are scattered all over this earth as strangers and aliens. Jesus tells us to

---

[33] John Piper, *Let the Nations Be Glad!: The Supremacy of God in Missions* (Kindle Locations 431-438), Baker Publishing Group, Kindle Edition.

store up wealth in our homeland, not in the land of our pilgrimage. We are not to store up treasures on earth but in heaven. What does it look like to store up heavenly treasure? We allow earthly treasure to flow through us in agreement with the fulfillment of God's mission. Part of how the Lord expands His kingdom is through those who do not see time, money, or possessions as theirs to hoard and do with as they will; rather these things are completely the Lord's and should be employed as He says, trusting that He will provide all that is needed (Matthew 6:33). He takes care of the birds and the lilies. We can trust Him to take care of us as we trust and obey.

Our belief or lack of belief that we are in a war and that we as believers are on the same team is evident by what we do with time, resources, and money. It is an issue of who we are serving—our own interests or the King's. Jesus made clear that we cannot serve Him and be simultaneously devoted to earthly riches. In context Jesus was saying that we cannot depend on money or anything else to meet our needs while we are depending on Him.

There are eternal implications for what we do with money and all the resources given to us. We are making earthly investments or heavenly investments (Matthew 6:19-20). Our investments focus on what the inner person is focused on, the temporary or the eternal, the mission of God or the building of our own kingdom (Matthew 6:21-23; 2 Corinthians 4:16-18). Repeatedly, the truth laid out in Scripture is that we can store up treasure on earth and it will amount to nothing in eternity, or we can store up for ourselves treasure in heaven that will last for eternity (Matthew 6:19-24; Philippians 4:17; 1 Timothy 6:19). The key is not whether we have a little or a lot in earthly accounts. It is the heart motivation and action connected to these accounts—the spread of God's mission or the "security" of our own lives. Concerning eternal implications of how we steward resources, Randy Alcorn writes, "I believe [eternity] is the primary missing ingredient in most Christian books on finances. When we look at money only as our money, and not in light of its impact on eternity, we walk away with a cloudy and shortsighted vision that results in cloudy and shortsighted financial decisions and lifestyles."[34]

---

[34] Randy Alcorn, *Money, Possessions, and Eternity* (Kindle Location 461-463), Tyndale House Publishers, Kindle Edition.

In relation to Matthew 6:20's "lay up for yourselves treasures," Randy Alcorn comments, "'For yourselves.' Does it seem strange that Jesus commands us to do what's in our own best interest? Isn't that selfish? No— God expects and commands us to act out of enlightened self-interest. Our generosity is not only for God's own glory, not only for others' good, but also for our good. Selfishness is when we pursue gain at the expense of others. But God doesn't have a limited number of treasures to distribute. When you store up treasures for yourself in heaven, it doesn't reduce the treasures available to others. In fact, it is by serving God and others that we store up heavenly treasures. Everyone gains; no one loses."[35]

As we see the extravagance of Jesus and that He is pleased to give us the kingdom, we will abide in Him and agree with Him for the necessary resources to finish the mission.

We will give with open hands to the extent that we see the openness of God's own hand in giving up His Son for us (Psalm 145:16; Romans 8:32). The earth is the Lord's and the fullness thereof (Psalm 24:1). He has unbounded resources. God continually gives and thoroughly enjoys doing so. As Jesus articulated, "It is more blessed to give than to receive" (Acts 20:35). As we abide in Jesus, He will lead us to give and He will return more to us.

We are able to freely give as we know we have been freely given the greatest treasure of all. The Father gave us Jesus, the One through whom we were created, who has provided our redemption and has all authority in heaven and on earth. Having Jesus, we have ultimate treasure.

So what is your treasure? A. W. Tozer posed four questions to help us discover the answer. "What do we value most? What would we most hate to lose? What do our thoughts turn to most frequently when we are free to think of what we will? And finally, what affords us the greatest pleasure?"[36]

Go back and consider each question personally. When we do not believe that eternity is our home and Jesus is our life, we will not focus properly. Our focus will be on the present and our mere 70-80 years. How pathetic when

---

[35] Randy Alcorn, *Money, Possessions, and Eternity* (Kindle Locations 2234-2238), Tyndale House Publishers, Kindle Edition.
[36] Ibid. (Kindle Locations 2125-2135).

these years are actually the arena where we prepare for eternity (2 Corinthians 5:10; 1 Corinthians 3:10-14). Why invest our all into what is fading away?

John Wesley and David Livingstone were men who saw properly. John Wesley said, "I value things only by the price they shall gain in eternity."[37] David Livingstone said, "I place no value on anything I possess, except in relation to the kingdom of God."[38] They found the treasure hidden in the field and thus were able to make a paradigm change in how they saw money and possessions (Matthew 13:44).

As ambassadors of Christ, we should be intently focused on the dream of His heart and be faithful stewards with worldly goods, using them for eternal purposes, according to the commander's direction. Jesus instructed us on how to use the good of this world: "Make friends for yourselves by unrighteous mammon [wealth], that when you fail, they may receive you into an everlasting home. He who is faithful in what is least is faithful also in much; and he who is unjust in what is least is unjust also in much. Therefore if you have not been faithful in the unrighteous mammon, who will commit to your trust the true riches? And if you have not been faithful in what is another man's, who will give you what is your own? No servant can serve two masters; for either he will hate the one and love the other, or else he will be loyal to the one and despise the other. You cannot serve God and mammon" (Luke 16:9b-13). Let us be those who are rich toward God with earthly goods, using them to build the church.

Sadly, looking at statistics, one can only wonder how on board we are with God's dream, and where we are deceived about the purpose of material blessing. Statistics can be up for debate and may differ some here and there but even if they differed 10% in the positive, the present scenario is still not pleasant. On the positive side, God is building His church. The gospel has been going forth in recent times like a flood across the nations. Seeking to reach the unreached is growing as a church focus. But sadly, of foreign mission funding, 87% goes for work among those already Christian. 12%

---

[37] Ibid. (Kindle Locations 2152).
[38] Ibid.

goes to work among those already evangelized, though non-Christian. 1% goes for work among the unevangelized and unreached people.[39]

Here are some observations: "Evangelical Christians could provide all of the funds needed to plant a church in each of the 6,900 unreached people groups with only 0.03% of their income. The Church has roughly 3,000 times the financial resources and 9,000 times the manpower needed to finish the Great Commission. If every evangelical gave 10% of their income to missions we could easily support 2 million new missionaries."[40] If this is the case, what is holding back the resources for finishing the task?

Dalton Thomas comments, "Tragically, at this point, frontier missions is simply not a priority to most in the Western church. We invest less than 1% of our resources into ministry to unreached people groups. This means that either God is unconcerned about the issue (which leaves Him responsible for the near wholesale avoidance of these people), or it is we who are indifferent (which places the guilt of negligence upon us)...One missions organization puts it this way: 'If everyone is obeying God's "calling" to be a missionary wherever they are then God is calling 99.9995% of people to work among the 44.3% of the world population that already has the gospel, and calling virtually no one (.0005%) to relocate among the other 53.7% of the world population that are not Christian. You have a better chance of being in a plane crash than being one of the 2 billion Christians in the world that are [Unreached People Groups] missionaries.' The fact that we in the West are so unconcerned about the unreached and unengaged is an injustice of epic proportions.

"Still, after two thousand years, half of the Earth's population has never met an ambassador for Christ! In the book The Spiritual Secret of Hudson Taylor, the son and daughter-in-law of the frontier missionary recall the story of an interaction between Taylor and a new and deeply grateful Chinese convert. The new believer...unexpectedly raised the question: 'How long have you had the Glad Tidings in your country?' 'Some hundreds of years,' was the reluctant reply [from Taylor]. 'What! Hundreds of years? My father

---

[39] Mark R. Baxter, *The Coming Revolution: Because Status Quo Missions Won't Finish the Job* (Tate Publishing, 2007).

[40] "Missions Stats," The Traveling Team, http://www.thetravelingteam.org/stats/.

sought the Truth,' he continued sadly, 'and died without finding it. Oh, why did you not come sooner?' It was a moment, the pain of which Hudson Taylor could never forget, and which deepened his earnestness in seeking to bring Christ to those who might still be reached...

"The question posed to Taylor stands as an indictment of the church in our generation, and as a challenge to every believer. Why have so few gone? Why are there still so many unreached peoples? Why are there no laborers in so many fields that are ripe for harvest? The answer to these questions is simple: fear. Fear of loss, fear of pain, fear of death. To embrace the call to frontier missions, we must first be freed from the bondage of fear."[41]

These words focus more on why laborers have not gone out and less on resources to fund them, but the issue of fear is the same. We resist sending resources because we are afraid of lack. Yet God has given the clear promise, written through Paul, "He who sows sparingly will also reap sparingly, and he who sows bountifully will also reap bountifully. So let each one give as he purposes in his heart, not grudgingly or of necessity; for God loves a cheerful giver. And God is able to make all grace abound toward you, that you, always having all sufficiency in all things, may have an abundance for every good work. As it is written: 'He has dispersed abroad, He has given to the poor; His righteousness endures forever.' Now may He who supplies seed to the sower, and bread for food, supply and multiply the seed you have sown and increase the fruits of your righteousness, while you are enriched in everything for all liberality, which causes thanksgiving through us to God" (2 Corinthians 9:6b-11). As we give, the Lord's grace abounds to us, and we receive more to release. Releasing resources makes a way for releasing the gospel and bringing people out of the kingdom of darkness into the kingdom of light. So truly, our giving through God's grace has eternal implications. We can use possessions in a way that they last temporarily, or eternally.

The spread of the gospel does not happen by chance. The spread of the gospel in Jesus' day and in the early church happened through people willingly giving time, money, and resources. To advance nearly anything in life, willingness and follow through are required. Let us give ourselves fully to that which will never pass away. Resources are essential, along with raising missional awareness in the global church. Without consistent

---

[41] Dalton Thomas, *Unto Death: Martyrdom, Missions, and the Maturity of the Church* (Kindle Locations 774-789, 792-795), Maskilim Publishing, Kindle Edition.

teaching and reminders of the mission, prayer diminishes, laborers decrease, and resources dwindle. In the next chapter, we will look at training the church to stay focused on the mission.

Ben Melancon

Chapter 15

Training the Church

Training is an essential part of ongoing success for any group of people moving together toward a shared goal. Values the group cherish and live by, along with an ongoing focus on the shared desire, must be instilled in the training. For example, a country's government, through educating the upcoming generation and through various news outlets, raises awareness of the values and history of that nation and the potential threats to those values from other nations. As a result, people sign up, and in some cases are required to go into the military to defend the country.

Concerning the kingdom of God, the church is supposed to be gathered around the shared desire of loving God the way He loves us and loving our neighbors as ourselves. We value such things as righteousness, purity of heart, meekness, being merciful, etc. as we move together. From our shared desire and moving in Jesus' values, we work with Him to finish the mission of declaring the gospel to the ends of the earth until every tribe has heard. Thus, this value should be a driving force or main pillar in the church wherever gathered. The church is to raise awareness of the eternal plan of God, the values of His kingdom, and His commission to preach His kingdom to all peoples. For the church to raise awareness, we must know the mission and be filled with passion for its fulfillment.

Through the cross, Jesus reestablished the dominion that Adam and Eve lost. In military terms, He went on the offensive, because of love, into enemy territory to secure what rightfully belongs to Him. He calls His church to go on the offensive with Him into all regions of the earth and usher people from the power of Satan to the power of God through the preaching of the gospel.

As citizens of the kingdom of heaven and strangers in this present world, we have "signed up" to be in God's army. We live in a battlefield and the war will not be over until every tribe has heard the gospel and Jesus returns. How can people know how to be a part of this offensive if they are not told about

Jesus' global mission? This is like having an army without a clear objective. For the church to work together as many individual parts, while not overly focusing on their individual parts at the expense of the whole, the church must have God's story in front of them, as well as where we are in the story, and what is left to accomplish.

There are various reasons why the local church does not emphasize God's global purpose. Some do not have the big picture of God's story clear in their minds as laid out in the Scriptures. Some shepherds do not see the value of their own congregations being involved. Some see it as people being taken from their congregation and local work. Some see it as too costly. They forget or refuse to accept that they too were once lost and the Great Shepherd reached out to them from heaven as He came to earth. When the local church does not raise awareness of the global mission, they prohibit members from sharing the wonder of inviting those from all peoples to the wedding feast of the Son (Matthew 22:1-14).

Some do not see why it is necessary for some from their own flock to go to unreached places. "Isn't there too much work to do at home?" There is always work. And there are multitudes of Bibles sitting unused, church parking lots that lie empty multiple days a week, and citizens of the kingdom of God focused more on building programs, recreational activities, and bank accounts while billions languish day and night with no Bible, no churches, and no saints to invite them to the wedding banquet. As Jim Elliot prepared to go to Ecuador's unreached, some believed that he would be more useful in his "native land." He responded, "I dare not stay home while Quichuas perish. What if the well-filled church in the homeland needs stirring? They have the Scriptures, Moses, and the prophets, and a whole lot more. Their condemnation is written on their bank books and in the dust on their Bible covers."[42]

The responsibility to work with Jesus to finish His mission is on every congregation of believers, not just a few. A parable written by James M. Weber, who was a missionary to Japan, gives a clear picture of this, including the many jobs necessary in the operation:

---

[42] Elisabeth Elliot, *Through Gates of Splendor* (Kindle Locations 166-168), Tyndale House Publishers, Kindle Edition.

There was an apple grower who had acres and acres of apple trees. In all, he had 10,000 acres of apple orchards. One day he went to the nearby town. There, he hired 1,000 apple pickers. He told them:

"Go to my orchards. Harvest the ripe apples, and build storage buildings for them so that they will not spoil. I need to be gone for a while, but I will provide all you will need to complete the task. When I return, I will reward you for your work. I'll set up a Society for the Picking of Apples. The Society— to which you will all belong—will be responsible for the entire operation. Naturally, in addition to those of you doing the actual harvesting, some will carry supplies, others will care for the physical needs of the group, and still others will have administrative responsibilities."

As he set up the Society structure, some people volunteered to be pickers and others to be packers. Others put their skills to work as truck drivers, cooks, accountants, storehouse builders, apple inspectors and administrators. Every one of his workers could, of course, have picked apples. In the end, however, only 100 of the 1,000 employees wound up as full-time pickers.

The 100 pickers started harvesting immediately. Ninety-four of them began picking around the homestead. The remaining six looked out toward the horizon. They decided to head out to the far-away orchards.

Before long, the storehouses in the 800 acres immediately surrounding the homestead had been filled by the 94 pickers with beautiful, delicious apples.

The orchards on the 800 acres around the homestead had thousands of apple trees. But with almost all of the pickers concentrating on them, those trees were soon picked nearly bare. In fact, the ninety-four apple pickers working around the homestead began having difficulty finding trees which had not been picked.

As the apple picking slowed down around the homestead, Society members began channeling effort into building larger storehouses and developing better equipment for picking and packing. They even started some schools to train prospective apple pickers to replace those who one day would be too old to pick apples.

Sadly, those ninety-four pickers working around the homestead began fighting among themselves. Incredible as it may sound, some began stealing apples that had already been picked. Although there were enough trees on the 10,000 acres to keep every available worker busy, those working nearest the homestead failed to move into unharvested areas. They just kept working those 800 acres nearest the house. Some on the northern edge sent their trucks to get apples on the southern side. And those on the south side sent their trucks to gather on the east side.

Even with all that activity, the harvest on the remaining 9,200 acres was left to just six pickers. Those six were, of course, far too few to gather all the ripe fruit in those thousands of acres. So, by the hundreds of thousands, apples rotted on the trees and fell to the ground.

One of the students at the apple-picking school showed a special talent for picking apples quickly and effectively. When he heard about the thousands of acres of untouched faraway orchards, he started talking about going there.

His friends discouraged him. They said: "Your talents and abilities make you very valuable around the homestead. You'd be wasting your talents out there. Your gifts can help us harvest apples from the trees on our central 800 acres more rapidly. That will give us more time to build bigger and better storehouses. Perhaps you could even help us devise better ways to use our big storehouses since we have wound up with more space than we need for the present crop of apples."

With so many workers and so few trees, the pickers and packers and truck drivers—and all the rest of the Society for the Picking of Apples living around the homestead—had time for more than just picking apples.

They built nice houses and raised their standard of living. Some became very conscious of clothing styles. Thus, when the six pickers from the far-off orchards returned to the homestead for a visit, it was apparent that they were not keeping up with the styles in vogue with the other apple pickers and packers.

To be sure, those on the homestead were always good to those six who worked in the far away orchards. When any of those six returned from the far away fields, they were given the red carpet treatment. Nonetheless, those six pickers were saddened that the Society of the Picking of Apples spent 96 percent of its budget for bigger and better apple-picking methods and equipment and personnel for the 800 acres around the homestead while it spent only 4 percent of its budget on all those distant orchards.

To be sure, those six pickers knew that an apple is an apple wherever it [is] picked. They knew that the apples around the homestead were just as important as apples far away. Still, they could not erase from their minds the sight of thousands of trees which had never been touched by a picker.

They longed for more pickers to come help them. They longed for help from packers, truck drivers, supervisors, equipment-maintenance men, and ladder builders. They wondered if the professionals working back around the homestead could teach them better apple-picking methods so that, out where they worked, fewer apples would rot and fall to the ground.

Those six sometimes wondered to themselves whether or not the Society for the Picking of Apples was doing what the orchard owner had asked it to do.

While one might question whether the Society was doing all the owner wanted done, the members did keep very busy. Several members were convinced that proper apple picking requires nothing less than the very best equipment. Thus, the Society assigned several members to develop bigger and better ladders as well as nicer boxes to store apples. The Society also prided itself at having raised the qualification level for full-time apple pickers.

When the owner returns, the Society members will crowd around him. They'll proudly show off the bigger and better ladders they've built and the nice apple boxes they've designed and made. One wonders how happy that owner will be, however, when he looks out and sees the acres and acres of untouched trees with their unpicked apples.[43]

The harvest truly is great and the workers are few, just as Jesus said. Let's use the apple orchard example with the current scenario to give a view of where we are in finishing world evangelization. Imagine the earth as the 10,000 acres of apples. Around 40% of the apple orchards have little to no workers among them. Of around four million people who are employed in full-time ministry, only around two hundred thousand are working among the unreached 40%. Among the people who do other jobs to aid the work of those in full time ministry, most of the efforts focus on the 60% of the apple orchards where Bibles and churches already exist. Only around 1% of financial resources being put into the mission are focused on the 40% that remain unreached. Though most focus on the 6,000 acres already reached, Jesus is focused on having all

---

[43] James M. Weber. "Orchard Parable: The Society for the Picking of Apples." Edited by Howard Culbertson. Southern Nazarene University, http://home.snu.edu/~hculbert/apples.htm.

10,000 acres. Let us not limit the "few workers" by not focusing on Jesus' dream for all nations to be His inheritance, and being willing to do what He wants to do with us, and go with Him where He wants to go through us.

A legitimate question arises: Why should we be so concerned about going to the unreached, and not stay in our "native land"? In North Africa, there is one Christian pastor or missionary for every two million people. If the ratio of Christian workers to the total population that is in North Africa were applied to the U.S. and Canada, those two countries would have about 120 full-time Christian workers living in them.[44]

Though Jesus had a specific assignment to the unreached peoples of Israel, His focus was global. Since Jesus' focus is on every tribe, shouldn't this be our focus? As we abide in Jesus, we can fulfill our specific assignment while having a global focus, seeing ourselves as part of a team with one mission to invite all peoples to partake in the wedding feast. Let us not hinder those who should fill a specific assignment to go to the unreached. May we openly declare Jesus' vision and goal, and invite Him to work in our hearts, that we would pray, go, train, care for those who mobilize, and let resources flow through us.

Nate Saint is helpful here: "It is not the call of the needy thousands, rather it is the simple intimate [fact] of the prophetic Word that there shall be some from every tribe in His presence in the last day and in our hearts we feel that it is pleasing to Him that we should interest ourselves in making an opening into the Auca (people group) prison for Christ…Would that we could comprehend the lot of these stone-age people who live in mortal fear of ambush on the jungle trail…those to whom the bark of a gun means sudden, mysterious death…those who think all men in all the world are killers like themselves. If God would grant us the vision, the word sacrifice would disappear from our lips and thoughts; we would hate the things that seem now so dear to us; our lives would suddenly be too short, we would despise time-robbing distractions and charge the enemy with all our energies in the name of Christ. May God help us to judge ourselves by the eternities that separate the Aucas from a comprehension of Christmas and Him, who, though He was rich, yet for our sakes became poor so that we might, through His poverty, be made rich. 'Lord, God, speak to my

---

own heart and give me to know Thy Holy will and the joy of walking in it. Amen.'"[45]

In Part 3, we have looked at four major ways you can be involved in God's mission as you abide in His love. Now that you have a picture of God's story, know the dream of His heart, and His command to make disciples of all people groups, how is God calling you to respond? With Jesus as your supreme treasure, what is the part you play in going, praying, sending resources, and raising awareness?

Words from David Platt fitfully summarize the past few chapters: "What happens when radical obedience to Christ becomes the new normal? Are you willing to see? You have a choice. You can cling to short-term treasures that you cannot keep, or you can live for long-term treasures that you cannot lose: people coming to Christ…[and] unreached tribes receiving the gospel. And the all consuming satisfaction of knowing and experiencing Christ as the treasure above all others. You and I have an average of about 70 or 80 years on this earth. During these years we are bombarded with the temporary. Make money. Get stuff. Be comfortable…Have fun. In the middle of it all, we get blinded to the eternal. But it's there. You and I stand on the porch of eternity. Both of us will soon stand before God to give an account for our stewardship of the time, the resources, the gifts, and ultimately the gospel he has entrusted to us. When that day comes, I am convinced we will not wish we had given more of ourselves to the American dream [or any dream other than God's]. We will not wish we had made more money, acquired more stuff, lived more comfortably, taken more vacations, watched more television, pursued greater retirement, or been more successful in the eyes of this world. Instead we will wish we had given more of ourselves to living for the day when every nation, tribe, people, and language will bow around the throne and sing the praises of the Savior who delights in radical obedience and the God who deserves eternal worship. Are you ready to live for this dream? Let's not waver any longer."[46]

---

[45] Elisabeth Elliot, *Through Gates of Splendor* (Kindle Locations 2034-2052), Tyndale House Publishers, Kindle Edition.
[46] David Platt, *Radical: Taking Back Your Faith from the American Dream,* (Kindle Locations 2744-2757), The Crown Publishing Group. Kindle Edition.

Ben Melancon

Conclusion

I enjoy taking long walks in the woods. This is one of the primary ways I draw near to the Lord. I have been doing this for 15 or so years, starting in my early to mid-twenties. One of my favorite places to do this is the property of the college I attended. Periodically I return there to walk.

On one of my recent treks, I noticed a few gates around the park were open that I had not seen open in the past. I did not think anything about this at first. However, after seeing a couple of gates open, I sensed the Lord saying, "The gates are open." I began to repeat this phrase periodically as I walked through the woods and I was reminded of something I wrote around the same time I started taking walks there. I titled what I wrote, "Contending at the Gates." The Lord, in that season, was revealing to me the battle that takes place in the spiritual realm and how intercession turns back the battle at the gates. Gates, especially in history, including biblical times, speak of places of authority where people are allowed to pass or not pass.

I continued to wait in the Lord's presence as I walked, to see what He was saying. I sensed Him saying that over the past 12 years (this was a few years ago), due to the corporate prayers of the saints night and day around the globe, there has been a victory in the heavenly realms. The gates are now open for the finishing of the Great Commission that Jesus gave. They are open because of concerted intercessory agreement with Jesus' victory at the cross (Colossians 2:13-15). The prayers of the saints have prevailed for the gospel to reach the remaining unreached peoples.

The gospel will go forth swiftly, and in a variety of ways. It may seem like gates are closed—that access is denied to many remaining groups. But spiritually, they are open. They will open physically where they currently seem closed, because of being opened in the spiritual realm through intercession. Some physical openings will come through various events that Jesus mentioned in Matthew 24 that happen in the generation leading up to His second coming. Jesus likened these signs to birth pains of a woman in labor. An example is earthquakes. Earthquakes in South Asia have opened physical gates to regions where outsiders were not previously welcomed. Another example is through tribes being pushed out and living in refugee camps. This happened to the Yazidi people in Iraq as ISIS pushed them out of their homeland. This devastation has actually provided a context where the Yazidi are being reached with the gospel. What the enemy intends for harm, God is more than able to use for good.

The Lord has spoken of the battle at the gates since the days of Abraham. Following Abraham's willingness to sacrifice Isaac, the Lord told Abraham: "By Myself I have sworn, says the LORD, because you have done this thing, and have not withheld your son, your only son— blessing I will bless you, and multiplying I will multiply your descendants as the stars of the heaven and as the sand which is on the seashore; and your descendants shall possess the gate of their enemies" (Genesis 22:16-17). Issac's wife Rebekah received similar words:

> *They blessed Rebekah and said to her: "Our sister, may you become the mother of thousands of ten thousands; and may your descendants possess the gates of those who hate them."* (Genesis 24:60)

The promise given to Abraham included physical land, a seed (heir), and all peoples being blessed through that seed. I believe the descendants refer to all who choose to be of the faith of Abraham from among all nations (Romans 4:13-17). When people follow in Abraham's footsteps, the world hates them. Some from every people will follow in his footsteps and possess the gates of those who hated them.

The theme of gates and the promises surfaced again in a dream that was given to Abraham's grandson Jacob (Genesis 28:12-17). In the dream he saw a ladder stretching from heaven to earth, with the Lord at the top of the ladder. Angels were going up and down the ladder. The Lord spoke to Jacob and promised him the land he was in during the dream, and promised that from Jacob's seed, all peoples will be blessed. Jacob declared what he saw as the house of God and the gate of heaven. At the beginning of His ministry, Jesus referenced this dream and declared Himself to be the house of God (John 1:51; 2:19-21). He is the gate through whom heaven and earth are brought together (Ephesians 1:9-10; John 10:9, 16). God's house is composed spiritually of some from every people on earth (Hebrews 3:6). Israel is the location of the physical house of God where Jesus will reign over the whole earth when He returns at the invitation from people of every tribe (Jeremiah 3:17; Ezekiel 43:7).

Jesus is presently building His corporate dwelling place among every people (Ephesians 2:22). He is building His church on the revelation of Himself as the Christ, the Son of the Living God, and He said the gates of Hades will not prevail against building His church (Matthew 16:16-18). The gates of Hades are a reference to the authority of the kingdom of darkness to hold men under its deceptive sway of bondage to sin and death. Through His death and resurrection, Jesus has all authority in heaven and on earth, He is alive forever and He holds the keys to Hades and Death (Revelation 1:17-18). He is in the business of possessing the gates of His enemies through His church as they abide in Him and complete His mission with Him.

Concerning building His church, Jesus gave us the privilege of partnering with Him. Jesus told Peter He would give him the keys of the kingdom of heaven, and in these keys, power to release God's activities and bind the kingdom of darkness' activities (Matthew 16:19). He spoke this in direct correlation to building His church—the spread of the gospel to every people. He invited Peter into the power of agreement with God's plan of giving Jesus all nations as His inheritance. Jesus gives us the keys of the kingdom by giving us revelation of Himself as the Christ. Potentially, the first line of the book of Revelation, "The Revelation of Jesus Christ," references what Jesus said to Peter concerning building the church on the revelation of Himself. When some from every people come to Jesus, then the end comes (Matthew 24:14). The book of Revelation shows the effect of intercession that moves mountains on earth and defeats the kingdom of darkness (Revelation 6:9-17; 8-9; 11:15). The church will truly possess the gates of her enemies.

The house of God is composed of Jew and Gentile, of many people from different languages and cultures, who have been brought out of the kingdom of darkness into the kingdom of light. In the Old Testament, Solomon and Zechariah prophesied of the Lord building His house in His strength, not people building in their strength (Psalm 127; Zechariah 4:6). Building the church does not happen through human strength. What Solomon was likely thinking of when he wrote Psalm 127 was the task he was given to build the temple in Jerusalem. I believe he was also prophesying of Jesus building His church and the gates of Hades not prevailing against it:

Unless the LORD builds the house, They labor in vain who build it; unless the LORD guards the city, the watchman stays awake in vain. [2]It is vain for you to rise up early, to sit up late, to eat the bread of sorrows; for so He gives His beloved sleep.

[3]Behold, children are a heritage from the LORD, The fruit of the womb is a reward. [4]Like arrows in the hand of a warrior, so are the children of one's youth. [5]Happy is the man who has his quiver full of them; they shall not be ashamed, but shall speak with their enemies in the gate. (Psalm 127:1-5)

Contending with enemies in the gate takes place in the context of night and day prayer. Solomon was building the physical temple to house the ark and to have night and day worship around God's dwelling place, as his father David instituted.

"Children of one's youth" is a powerful statement when in the context of believers born as new creations in Christ. The church is brought forth out of the kingdom of this world into the kingdom of God because of Jesus' sacrifice. David prophesied of Jesus receiving the dew of His youth in the day of His power (Psalm 110:3). By the time of His second coming, some from all peoples will have voluntarily received Jesus' goodness and He will have the nations as His inheritance (Psalm 2:8). Truly, He will see the labor of His soul and be satisfied (Isaiah 53:11). The church, as the dew of Jesus' youth, will silence the foe by their praise arising from the ends of the earth (Psalm 8:2; Isaiah 24:14-16). Dominion will be restored to people in fellowship with their Maker and the Lord's name will be known as excellent in all the earth (Psalm 8; 145; 149).

There is a generation in which some from all people groups will globally seek the God of Israel—the God of the whole earth. I believe David prophesied of this. He declared that the earth and all that is in it belongs to the Lord (Psalm 24:1-2). The question then arises, in the next verse, "Who may ascend the hill of the LORD? Or who may stand in His holy place?" The answer is:

[4]He who has clean hands and a pure heart, who has not lifted up his soul to an idol, nor sworn deceitfully. [5]He shall receive blessing from the LORD, And righteousness from the God of his salvation.

⁶This is Jacob, the generation of those who seek Him, who seek Your face. (Psalm 24:4-6)

The scene given is some from all people groups seeking the face of the one true God, not idols. Some from all peoples will ascend the hill of the Lord to appear at His throne of grace through the blood of Jesus, and when this happens, it will be time for the kingdom of this world to come under the reign of Christ (Revelation 11:15; Matthew 6:9-10). When this occurs, it will be time for the King of glory to come to earth. David finished the Psalm by declaring, "Lift up your heads, O you gates [every place of authority on earth – Colossians 1:16]! And be lifted up, you everlasting doors! And the King of glory shall come in. Who is this King of glory? The LORD strong and mighty, [t]he LORD mighty in battle. Lift up your heads, O you gates! Lift up, you everlasting doors! And the King of glory shall come in. Who is this King of glory? The LORD of hosts, He is the King of glory" (Psalm 24:7-10). Through His church's agreement on earth, Jesus will have earthly preeminence as He has it in heaven (Ephesians 1:22-23; 3:10-11; Colossians 1:18).

The gates are open and as the church prays night and day unto the return of Jesus and the establishment of Jerusalem as the praise of the earth, she will pass through the gates of every people on earth, proclaiming the gospel of the kingdom. Jesus is returning and all will see the glory of the Lord (Isaiah 40:5). Through prayer, the word of the Lord will go forth and Jesus will return. As Isaiah prophesied:

⁷How beautiful upon the mountains are the feet of him who brings good news [laborers across the earth], who proclaims peace, Who brings glad tidings of good things, who proclaims salvation, Who says to Zion, "Your God reigns!" ⁸Your watchmen [those who pray – Isaiah 62:6-7] shall lift up their voices, with their voices they shall sing together; for they shall see eye to eye when the LORD brings back Zion. ⁹Break forth into joy, sing together, you waste places of Jerusalem! For the LORD has comforted His people, He has redeemed Jerusalem. ¹⁰The LORD has made bare His holy arm in the eyes of all the nations; and all the ends of the earth shall see the salvation of our God. (Isaiah 52:7-10)

The following poem from a friend, Evie Palmer, that gives a fitful summary for this book:

Great Commission Poem

Through the setting of dynamic worship and prayer
I spoke to my saints through a whisper in their ear
I reminded them of my harvest, and the fruit of my reward
That I long to return, but laborers must go forth
These believers were stirred and commissioned, to go out to the nations
To finish the task of spreading my gospel message far and wide
To go out to the dark places, to every tribe, tongue and nation
To be ministers and flames of fire
To rebuild communities where prayer is at the center
To be a beacon of hope in this darkest hour
For the word of the Lord to go forth
However, Satan in his cunning tactics
Sent his weapon of fear to grip them to stay back
But when fear was demolished, he sent doubt their way
To keep these called out ones in their safe place
And when fear and doubt wouldn't do, he sent division a slew
To keep the word silent
But these warriors took up the shield of faith,
They battled doubt, discouragement, and dismay
And pushed through every obstacle in their way
They did not allow fear to grip them, or wars to come between them
But stood firm in their faith
They trusted in the word that was spoken, and believed what they heard
Which resulted in victory as they were launched to the ends of the earth
These sent out ones are preparing the way
For I [Jesus] am coming again, and coming quickly

Ben Melancon is available for book interviews and personal appearances. For more information contact Ben Melancon c/o Advantage Books at: info@advbooks.com

To purchase additional copies of these books, visit our bookstore at: www.advbookstore.com

Longwood, Florida, USA
"we bring dreams to life"™
www.advbookstore.com

Made in the USA
Columbia, SC
14 March 2024

33075266R00091